A NOTE FROM THE AKC

From Dennis B. Sprung
AKC President and CEO

Meet Your New Dog

Welcome to *Meet the German Shepherd*. Whether you're a long-time German Shepherd Dog owner, or you've just gotten your first puppy, we wish you a lifetime of happiness and enjoyment with your new pet.

In this book, you'll learn about the history of the breed, receive tips on feeding, grooming, and training, and learn about all the fun you can have with your dog. The American Kennel Club and BowTie Press hope that this book serves as a useful guide on the lifelong journey you'll take with your canine companion.

Owned and cherished by millions across America, German Shepherds make wonderful companions and also enjoy taking part in a variety of dog sports, including Conformation (dog shows), Obedience, Rally®, and Agility.

Thousands of GSDs have also earned the AKC Canine Good Citizen® certification by demonstrating their good manners at home and in the community. We hope that you and your German Shepherd will become involved in AKC events, too! Learn how to get involved at www.akc.org/events or find a training club in your area at www.akc.org/events/trainingclubs.cfm.

We encourage you to connect with other German Shepherd owners on the AKC website (www.akc.org), Facebook (www.facebook.com/americankennelclub), and Twitter (@akcdoglovers). Also visit the website for the German Shepherd Dog Club of America (www.gsdca.org), the national parent club for the German Shepherd, to learn about the breed from reputable exhibitors and breeders.

Enjoy *Meet the German Shepherd*!

Sincerely,

Dennis B. Sprung
AKC President and CEO

6

52

72

96

Contents

1. FALL IN LOVE WITH THE GERMAN SHEPHERD 6
2. THE GSD DESIGN 16
3. SHOPPING FOR A GERMAN SHEPHERD 28
4. YOUR DOG'S NEW HOME 40
5. SCHOOL DAYS 52
6. HOUSE-TRAINING YOUR GSD 62
7. HOME CARE FOR THE GSD 72
8. GSD COMMAND CENTRAL 86
9. STAYING HEALTHY 96
10. ACTIVITIES FOR GERMAN SHEPHERDS 106

RESOURCES 122

INDEX 126

CHAPTER ONE

Fall in Love with the German Shepherd

One of the world's most recognizable purebred dogs, the German Shepherd Dog defies description. The American Kennel Club classifies the breed in its Herding Group, but herding sheep and goats only represents one aspect of this multi-faceted working dog. Images of the heroic and noble German Shepherd, assisting soldiers in wartime or working side-by-side with rescue workers after the September 11th attacks on New York City's World

THE AMERICAN KENNEL CLUB'S
Meet the German Shepherd™

The Responsible Dog Owner's Handbook

AKC's Meet the Breeds Series

BOWTIE PRESS®
Irvine, California
A Division of BowTie, Inc.

An Official Publication of  The American Kennel Club

AMERICAN KENNEL CLUB™

Brought to you by The American Kennel Club and The German Shepherd Dog Club of America.

Lead Editor: Lindsay Hanks
Art Director: Cindy Kassebaum
Production Supervisor: Jessica Jaensch
Assistant Production Manager: Tracy Vogtman
Book Project Specialist: Karen Julian

Vice President, Chief Content Officer: June Kikuchi
Vice President, Kennel Club Books: Andrew DePrisco
BowTie Press: Jennifer Calvert, Amy Deputato, Lindsay Hanks, Karen Julian, Jarelle S. Stein

Photographs by: Alamy: 36, 51; Blackhawk Productions (Dwight Dyke): Cover, 4, 11, 22, 71, 72, 73, 75, 85, 90, 101, 105, 108, 116, 119; BowTie Studio: Cover, Back Cover, 8, 34, 42, 44, 56, 77, 124; Close Encounters of the Furry Kind: 1, 33, 57, 70, 83, 110; Diane Lewis: Cover, 4, 4, 6, 7, 19, 24, 25, 30, 48, 54, 62, 63, 66, 79, 89, 109, 117, 121; Fox Hill Photo: 12, 13, 14, 15, 26, 31, 32, 37, 38, 39, 40, 41, 43, 45, 49, 59, 61, 67, 68, 69, 74, 76, 78, 80, 81, 84, 88, 93, 94, 99, 102, 103, 113; Infocus by Miguel (Miguel Betancourt): 20, 21, 50, 115; Jerry Schulman: 4, 9, 10, 18, 35, 46, 64, 112; Mark Raycroft: Cover, 3, 16, 17, 27, 28, 29, 47, 52, 53, 55, 96-97, 106, 107, 111, 120; Shutterstock: 86, 87.

Copyright © 2011 The American Kennel Club and BowTie Press

BowTie Press®
Division of BOWTIE INC.
3 Burroughs, Irvine, CA 92618

All rights reserved. No part of this book may be reproduced, stored in a retrieval system, or transmitted in any form or by any means, electronic, mechanical, photocopying, recording, or otherwise, without the prior written permission of BowTie Press®, except for the inclusion of brief quotations in an acknowledged review.

Library of Congress Cataloging-in-Publication Data

The American Kennel Club's meet the German shepherd dog : the responsible dog owner's handbook.
    p. cm. -- (AKC's meet the breeds series)
 ISBN 978-1-935484-72-1
 1. German shepherd dog. I. American Kennel Club.
 SF429.G37A44 2012
 636.737'6--dc23
                    2011031433

Printed and bound in the United States
14 13 12 11 1 2 3 4 5 6 7 8 9 10

Dogs at Work

The GSD's intelligence and willingness to cooperate with humans make the breed versatile working dogs. They excel in the following jobs: guarding people and property; police and military service, including scent work such as bomb and drug detection; guiding the blind; search and rescue; and guarding and herding livestock.

Trade Center and the Pentagon are seared in the minds of Americans today, just as recollections of Rin Tin Tin and Strongheart on movie screens moved earlier generations.

What's not to love about the GSD, as the breed is commonly called? Is there a more courageous breed? The German Shepherd remains a fearless protector, a loyal and devoted pet, a trainable and intelligent competition dog, and one of the most versatile four-legged animals on the planet.

Since the breed's rise to prominence in the early 1900s, when canine Hollywood star Strongheart reigned on the silver screen, the German Shepherd has excelled in every imaginable area of canine duty: herding dog, military working dog, protection dog, law-enforcement K9, drug and bomb detector, guide and assistance dog, hearing dog, and, of course, search-and-rescue dog. In fact, when the American Kennel Club launched its DOGNY program to commemorate the hero dogs of September 11th, the German Shepherd was used as the statue model for the poignant artwork.

THE RIGHT DOG FOR YOU?

The temperament of this professional working dog doesn't automatically translate to "ideal family dog" in most people's minds. For all of the outstanding qualities that make the GSD a brilliant working and service dog, smitten potential owners must understand that this is an excessively bright animal who takes his job very seriously. Make no mistake: the German Shepherd Dog needs a job!

An unemployed GSD is a miserable companion. Left alone without something to do in the home or backyard, the GSD can become destructive, overly vocal, and generally unhappy. A lot of dog in terms of strength, intellect, and drive, the German Shepherd should never be left to his own creative devices. This family-oriented canine wants to be a part of his human pack, and he will thrive and become the ideal family dog he was meant to be when given plenty of exercise and human contact.

For all of the breed's intelligence, the German Shepherd cannot teach himself. This remarkable working canine does not instinctively know right from wrong, and without proper training and guidance, he does not know what is acceptable behavior. He still requires training and firm yet gentle and consistent handling by a master who is able to command the dog's respect. Confident breeds like the GSD require a strong leader, or they will intuitively sense any weakness and assume a dominant role, which is clearly undesirable when dealing with a breed as powerful as this.

A family with children will undoubtedly be well protected by a German Shepherd. The breed's innate maternal instincts apply to the family's children, and GSDs take their child-care duties as seriously as any other task assigned to them. When properly trained and socialized with children, the GSD is remarkably gentle and tolerant of children of all ages.

Before adding a German Shepherd to your family, you must consider all of the dog's needs—exercise, space, companionship, occupation, training,

Friendly and highly trainable, German Shepherds love to be where the action is with their owners.

and so forth—and make a commitment to providing for each of these needs. GSDs are handsome, friendly, and smart—qualities that make them appealing to many dog lovers who are not suited for this large, active, intelligent dog. Only responsible owners who are willing to provide for all of the GSD's needs should consider this breed. If you and your family meet those conditions, the German Shepherd will reward you with love and devotion.

COAT CARE

Dogs shed; it's just a matter of how much. The good news is that the German Shepherd's thick double coat only sheds a lot for about two weeks twice a year. The bad news is that the coat sheds a little every day of the other forty-eight weeks. Brushing becomes a necessary part of daily life.

The German Shepherd typically enjoys the attention he gets during grooming, and owners simply have to set aside five minutes a day to give their dogs a once-over. Likewise, ideal GSD owners must be less fussy about a ball of fuzz tumbling down the hallway or some stray hairs on your blouse or jeans. Just accept that you'll never have it 100 percent cleaned up.

In terms of the actual length, the GSD's coat is medium long, with a longer, thicker coat on the dog's neck and a longer coat on the dog's legs. Brushing keeps the dog's coat looking healthy and clean. Ideally, the hair on the body lies close

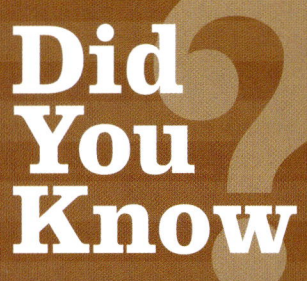

Did You Know?

The American Kennel Club began offering the modern Best in Show award in 1924. The first German Shepherd Dog to win a Best in Show was Ch. Etzel v.d. Ettersburg, who won the award on March 26, 1924.

Fall in Love with the German Shepherd

Thinking about getting a German Shepherd Dog? Make sure you have enough time and energy to dedicate to this active and fun-loving breed.

and is straight and harsh, though some shepherds have slightly wavy or wiry coats, too. A show dog's coat should never be soft, silky, wooly, or curly.

The GSD's thick double coat insulates the dog from heat and cold, enabling him to work in the most inclement weather. The outer hairs are water-resistant, and the thick underfur provides insulation in cold weather. Burrs and other clinging seeds brush right out of the coat. Coat color varies from black and tan to sable and gray sable. Solid white is not permitted on show dogs.

EMPLOYING THE GSD

Do you own a hobby farm? Have you wondered what it would be like to look out your kitchen window upon a small flock of Merino sheep? If so, then you have the ideal sheep herder in your German Shepherd. Most people first think of the GSD as a police dog rather than a farm dog, when in fact the breed excels at both and certainly knew ewes and rams long before it recognized criminals and victims.

The rural renaissance is alive and well across the United States, and hobby farms are sprouting up everywhere. The return to nature and instinct has swept up dog lovers, too, and natural foods and remedies for dogs have become more popular than ever. Likewise, the AKC has been offering instinct tests for various

Always the Bridesmaid

In 1925, the German Shepherd Dog reached the position of number-one dog in the United States—and remained at the top for three years—unseating the popular Boston Terrier that had been the number-one breed of the 1910s. Number-one status was never achieved again, though the breed was number six in the 1950s and remained in the top four breeds every decade since then. From 1963 through 1972, the GSD was number two but never came close to dethroning the Poodle from the number one position. Currently, the GSD is once again at the number two position, behind the Labrador Retriever, who has held the top spot for more than twenty years.

Fall in Love with the German Shepherd

breeds for many years. Herding dogs like the GSD can participate in herding tests and trials, simulated events that put the dog's innate herding skills to work.

HERD MENTALITY

How exactly does a herding dog herd? When most people hear the term "sheep-herding dog," they visualize a shepherd sending out his dog to round up the flock and bring it to a location he designates. Historically, this is not the type of herding that the German Shepherd performed.

There are three basic styles of GSD herding; each evolved based on the local circumstances that sheep farmers faced.

1. **Driving** is the most common herding type. Seen in sheepdog trials, it requires the dog to push stock through gates, pens, and chutes. In this style of herding, the shepherd does not lead the flock, and the dog works on commands.

2. In **Mustering**, the dog fetches stock from long distances and brings them back to the shepherd.

3. **Tending** is the herding technique that the GSD was originally meant to do, which involves managing large flocks grazing and moving in open settings. The dog acts as a living fence. Large European manors did not build actual

Familiar Faces

Some truly famous German Shepherds have graced our big screens over the years. When Hollywood dog trainer Larry Trimble and his friend, writer Jane Murfin, heard the about the GSD war dogs, they decided the breed was perfect for film work. In 1920, they searched Germany and chose a three-year-old, 125-pound, police-dog-trained male named Etzel von Oringer. Renamed Strongheart, this GSD starred in several silent movies, including such classics as Jack London's *Call of the Wild* (1921) and *White Fang* (1925). Strongheart was the first canine movie star.

Another GSD, rescued as a puppy from a bombed-out war dog kennel in Lorraine, France, soon out-did Strongheart. Corporal Lee Duncan managed to bring this pup (named Rin Tin Tin after a French toy) back to the United States and trained him as he had seen the war dogs trained. At a show in 1921, "Rinty" amazed the audience by broad-jumping 13½ feet. Darrell Zanuck saw this and paid Duncan $350 to film Rinty with his new camera. Before his death in 1932, Rinty made 26 movies for Warner Brothers and became a huge star, receiving 10,000 fan letters a week. Rinty's offspring have continued to act in movies and television. The Rin Tin Tin breeding program is now owned by Ms. Daphne Hereford, daughter of Ms. Jannettia Propps, who inherited the line from Duncan. To stay up to date with Rin Tin Tin, go to www.rintintin.com.

German Shepherds love being put to work, but they also enjoy a little down time and R&R with the people they love.

fences until the nineteenth century, thus herding dogs were used to oversee the pastures, which were adjacent to other areas such as woodlands, grain fields, vegetable gardens, and vineyards. The sheep were only allowed to graze on fallow fields (those that had been allowed to grow to stubble and grass), usually about 10 acres large and outlined with furrows. The shepherd led the sheep from the edges of the plots, and the dogs kept them on the path. They may have had to pass miles of growing crops on the way to pasture. Once the flock was settled on a fallow field, the dogs patrolled the land to keep them there.

    Because tending dogs do not work under direct command, they had to be quick-witted enough to adapt to changing circumstances and able to make

If you like lively, intelligent mid-sized dogs, the German Shepherd just might be the breed for you.

independent decisions. The job required them to be assertive enough to keep determined sheep (strong animals heavier than the dogs) from getting into areas beyond the nonexistent fences. They needed enough self-confidence and control to physically force potential escapees back into the group by gripping only their wool. Above all, the tending job required courage to protect the sheep from humans and animal predators, like wolves and bears.

Join the Club

The parent club of a canine breed is considered the expert on everything related to that breed of dog. It's responsible for safeguarding and promoting a particular dog breed. These national organizations are members of the American Kennel Club and are made up of knowledgeable breeders. Each parent club determines the breed standard, denoting the most desired traits of an ideal specimen of the breed, which the AKC then officially approves. The standard is used to guide breeding practices and competition judging. The parent club of the German Shepherd is the German Shepherd Dog Club of America. Learn more about the club at its website, www.gsdca.org.

WHAT A SPORT

Consistent with the breed's historical role as a tending dog, the German Shepherd is a true team player and excels when working independently or by his master's side. In fact, the GSD excels at his person's side in most any dog sport. Whether he's flying over a hurdle in an agility trial or executing a broad jump in an obedience trial, the well-trained GSD is a focused, professional athlete who thrives on pleasing his handler. Tracking is another sport at which German Shepherd Dogs have been excelling for many years. Relying on his nose and brain, the GSD is a natural tracker, and these skills have been applied to many of the breed's professional disciplines, such as search and rescue, arson and drug detection, border control, police trailing, and many others.

CANINE CONSIDERATION

The rest of this book will dive into everything important you need to know to find and care for a German Shepherd. It's a lifetime commitment, and not one to be taken lightly. So before you go looking for a breeder, make sure bringing a dog into your home is really what you want. Examine your home environment and lifestyle to make sure the lively and personable GSD is really the dog for you.

Then, once you're certain that the German Shepherd Dog is your ideal breed, don't just rush out and buy the first one you see. Take the time to study the breed. Do your research and know which GSD qualities to look for when meeting available litters; learn the best tactics for training and socialization; study what you can do to contribute to your pet's health and happiness; and discover the vast array of activities you can do to bond with your active dog. Now, let's get to it!

Having endeared himself to humans centuries ago for his devoted service in livestock fields, the GSD has won over recent generations in his civic services.

At a Glance ...

German Shepherds have been one of the most popular dog breeds for the majority of the past century.

Devoted and highly trainable, GSDs make great service animals, as well as family pets.

GSDs thrive when given a "job" to do, whether it is guarding the family at home or apprehending criminals alongside a police officer.

German Shepherds have an instinctive herding mentality—a skill that has endeared them to humans throughout the world for hundreds of years.

The possibilities are endless when considering what activities to involve your German Shepherd Dog in to keep him healthy, active, and happy.

CHAPTER TWO

The GSD Design

Impressive and harmoniously built, the German Shepherd Dog is regarded as one of the world's most recognizable dogs. At once, this dog is strong, agile, and well muscled, while also alert and full of life. Defying definition, the German Shepherd possesses nobility and quality.

Many of the words in the above paragraph come from the official breed standard of the GSD, but words are merely words. How do they come together to describe this wonderful breed?

For the Record

The German Shepherd Dog that lays claim to winning the most Best in Shows is Ch. Altana's Mystique, owned by Jane Firestone and handled by James Moses. With 275 BIS wins, Mystique is not only the top-winning GSD of all time, she's also the show dog with the most wins in American history, earning the Top Dog spot in 1993 and 1994. In 1993 alone, she amassed 116 BIS wins, more than any other dog in a single year.

The question we ask is: what makes a German Shepherd Dog look like a German Shepherd? It's not simply the dog's size, shape, angulation, or gait, but rather the combination of all of these essential features that together create an ideal representation of the breed. Written by the German Shepherd Dog Club of America (the breed's national parent club) and approved by the American Kennel Club, the breed standard serves as a blueprint for breeding and judging at conformation shows. In fact, the purpose of dog shows is to determine which dogs are best suited for breeding. It's absolutely critical for breeders and judges to have an accepted "ideal" so that all of the valued qualities of the breed will be preserved from generation to generation.

To emphasize that the German Shepherd is not just a pretty face in a shiny coat, the breed standard also describes this dog's working ability. In the section on temperament, the standard states that the GSD must be "fit and willing to serve in its capacity as a companion, watchdog, blind leader, herding dog, or guardian, whichever the circumstances command. The ideal dog is a working animal with an incorruptible character combined with body and gait suitable for the arduous work which constitutes its primary purpose."

The German Shepherd's working ability and temperament are just as important as the desired physical characteristics that the standard details. These traits as described in the breed standard are intended to preserve the true working character of the breed. Although the vast majority of modern GSDs do not work

in the same capacities as their herding-dog ancestors, they should still possess the ability and true spirit that distinguishes this versatile working breed.

HERDING COUSINS

The German Shepherd Dog belongs to the Herding Group, the category of dogs that includes the shepherd's assistants. The GSD is the most popular of these breeds in the United States, but other highly regarded and recognized breeds in this group include the Australian Shepherd, Border Collie, Collie, and Shetland Sheepdog. In appearance, the Herding breeds vary significantly, from the Pembroke Welsh Corgi and the mop-like Puli to the tousled Bearded Collie and the rough-coated Bouvier des Flandres. The GSD appears most similar to its Belgian herding cousins—the Belgian Malinois, Belgian Shepherd, and Belgian Tervuren, all of which excel in similar disciplines. All of the shepherd breeds were developed in continental Europe and were designed to work independently

German Shepherds possess a natural drive to herd other animals—or people if the job calls for it.

A PIECE OF HISTORY

The American Kennel Club registered the first German Shepherd Dog in 1908, a female by the name of Queen Switzerland, registration number 115006.

The GSD in Brief

COUNTRY OF ORIGIN:
Germany

ORIGINAL USE:
Herding sheep and other livestock

GROUP:
Herding

AVERAGE LIFE SPAN:
12 to 14 years

COAT:
Double coat of medium length, consisting of a dense outer coat with straight, harsh, and close-lying hair and soft undercoat.

COLOR:
Strong rich colors are preferred, including sable, black, and black and tan. Pale, washed out colors are undesirable, and white is disqualified from the show ring.

GROOMING:
Once or twice weekly brushings recommended; daily brushing required during twice-annual shedding periods. Bathe whenever necessary. Ears, teeth, and nails should be attended to weekly.

HEIGHT/WEIGHT:
Males, 24 to 26 inches at the shoulder; females, 22 to 24 inches.

TRAINABILITY:
Very high

PERSONALITY:
Confident and approachable; direct and fearless, not prone to indiscriminate friendships; willing to meet new people and to excel in role as companion and working dog.

ACTIVITY LEVEL:
High; thrives with a job to do, and can do just about anything!

GOOD WITH OTHER PETS:
Yes, with proper introductions and training.

NATIONAL BREED CLUB:
German Shepherd Dog Club of America; www.gsdca.org

RESCUE:
American German Shepherd Rescue Association; www.agsra.org

The German Shepherd is the most popular of the Herding Group dogs.

and alongside the shepherd to control, protect, and move—or herd—livestock such as sheep, goats, and cattle.

POPULAR FROM THE START

Unlike the histories of many dog breeds, the German Shepherd's genesis is well documented. When Max von Stephanitz decided to launch a standardized program for the ideal working sheepdog, he set his eyes and heart upon a canine named Hektor von Linkshein, whom he renamed Horand von Grafrath, and deemed him to be the foundation dog for his new breed, the Deutsche Schaferhund or German Shepherd Dog. So impressed with this hard-working herding dog was von Stephanitz that he founded the Verein für Deutsche Schäferhunde (SV), the German breed club. The SV went on to become the largest specialty club in the world; today it boasts 1,600 local clubs and almost 80,000 members. Von

Stephanitz made lasting and far-reaching strides with his new breed and was able to exert great influence over the German breeders thanks to the success of the SV.

The German Shepherd quickly became the "it" dog for both military and police work, as well as for families seeking companionship and protection. A decade into the breeding program, the GSD made its way to America and was recognized by the American Kennel Club in 1908.

SOCIAL BUTTERFLY

The best GSD owner's home and lifestyle should be able to accommodate a big, active dog. This breed wasn't built for apartment-dwelling. Having a large, securely fenced yard is a must, as it is much easier to provide the German Shepherd Dog with opportunities to exercise freely. However, a GSD can adapt to living in an apartment if his owner is willing to spend at least 30 minutes twice a day taking the dog for a brisk walk.

The German Shepherd is a working dog with a drive to get up and go. If not exercised enough, he will get out of shape both mentally and physically. In addition to the time spent exercising your dog, you must be willing to find an activity that you both enjoy doing, then do it on a regular basis. GSDs need a "job" to do; otherwise they get bored and unruly. When the dog is young, his job should be to attend obedience classes and practice daily. Later, there are many interesting and enjoyable activities to choose from.

The GSD will fit into any human social group, whether a single-owner household or a family with several children. In families, older children and spouses can take on some of the responsibility to keep the GSD busy and happy. If the children

A Visionary for the Blind

Dorothy Harrison Eustis (1886–1946) was born in Philadelphia and today is remembered as the founder of The Seeing Eye, the first school for guide dogs in the United States. The organization, founded in 1929, was based on principles Eustis observed at a school in Germany that trained dogs to assist blind veterans. For a while, Eustis bred German Shepherd Dogs in Switzerland. The use of assistance dogs was unknown in the United States during this period, and the mission and success of The Seeing Eye changed the lives of many visually impaired individuals. By the time Eustis died in 1946, more than 1,300 blind individuals had been matched with guide dogs. The success of The Seeing Eye (www.seeingeye.org), based in Morristown, New Jersey, has spawned other guide dog schools around the world. Today assistance dogs are used for many other disabilities, including hearing loss, epilepsy, autism, and more. Eustis's life is celebrated in the book *Independent Vision* by Miriam Ascarelli, published in 2010 by Purdue University Press.

If you own a farm of any size, the German Shepherd would make a wonderful addition to help keep your menagerie in order.

are instructed on "dog etiquette" (that is, how to interact with the GSD calmly and in a non-threatening manner), the dog will be a willing and devoted playmate, protecting the children with his life if necessary. With a large breed like the GSD, it is imperative that parents supervise all dog-child interactions. No dogs, even small ones, should be left alone with a young child, as accidents do happen.

OWNER SUITABILITY

Successful German Shepherd owners (meaning people who can raise a mentally and physically sound German Shepherd Dog for many years) have certain personality traits and characteristics in common. Emotional stability is a

Meet the German Shepherd and More!

AMERICAN KENNEL CLUB

A great place to see German Shepherd Dogs and more than 200 other dog and cat breeds is at AKC Meet the Breeds®, hosted by the American Kennel Club and presented by Pet Partners, Inc. Not only can you see dogs, cats, puppies, and kittens of all sizes, you can also talk to experts in each of the breeds. Meet the Breeds features demonstration rings to watch events with law enforcement K9s, grooming, agility, and obedience. You also can browse the more than 100 vendor booths for every imaginable product for you and your pet.

It's great fun for the whole family. Meet the Breeds takes place in the fall in New York City. For more information, check out www.meetthebreeds.com.

cornerstone of this breed's personality, and the dog thrives with an equally calm and levelheaded owner. You must be predictable to the dog, or he will become insecure, and the relationship will lack the necessary trust and result in the dog developing anxiety.

The German Shepherd works for approval and learns best when guided by positive rewards rather than being forced into a behavior, so the breed's ideal owner must also be capable of providing strong positive feedback for the dog. Although your dog would undoubtedly like to have you with him all day, he can easily adapt to a routine, if you work during the day and are away from home—just be sure to make an extra effort to share time with him each day. At least a few quality minutes of one-on-one interaction such as obedience work or games in the yard are vital if you want to remain closely bonded to your shepherd. The rest of the time, he will be content to lounge around in your sight, perhaps giving an occasional nose-nudge to solicit petting.

Bigger Is Not Always Better!

In the past hundred years that German Shepherd Dogs have been selected for work as police, military, and home guardians, the breed has increased in body size (both height and weight), compared to the original German sheep-tending dogs. The current standard for this breed calls for a mature dog between 24 and 26 inches at the top of the shoulders. Well-proportioned GSDs at that size weigh about 70 to 90 pounds. It takes up to three years for a GSD youngster to completely fill out his large frame, although pups reach adult height by about a year of age.

Today, over-sized GSDs are often advertised as desirable. Beware, though, that GSDs that are significantly larger than the standard recommends (and all dogs much over 100 pounds, for that matter) are much more susceptible to joint problems and generally do not live as long. Bigger is definitely not better.

GSD Breed Standard

OVERALL: The breed has a distinct personality marked by direct and fearless, but not hostile, expression, self-confidence and a certain aloofness that does not lend itself to immediate and indiscriminate friendships. The dog is poised, but when the occasion demands, eager and alert; both fit and willing to serve in its capacity as companion, watchdog, blind leader, herding dog, or guardian, whichever the circumstances may demand.

PROPORTION:
The German Shepherd Dog is longer than tall. The desirable long proportion is not derived from a long back, but from overall length with relation to height.

HEAD:
The head is noble, cleanly chiseled, strong without coarseness, and in proportion to the body. The expression keen, intelligent and composed. Ears are moderately pointed, in proportion to the skull, open toward the front, and carried erect when at attention, the ideal carriage being parallel to each other and perpendicular to the ground. The muzzle is long and strong, and its topline is parallel to the topline of the skull. Jaws are strongly developed.

NECK:
The neck is strong and muscular, clean-cut and relatively long, proportionate in size to the head and without loose folds of skin. At attention, the head is raised and neck carried high; otherwise head is forward rather than up.

TOPLINE:
The withers are higher than and sloping into the level back. The back is straight, very strongly developed without sag or roach, and relatively short.

CHEST:
It is well filled and carried well down between the legs. It is deep and capacious, never shallow, with ample room for lungs and heart, Correct ribbing allows the elbows to move back freely when the dog is at a trot.

TAIL:
The tail is bushy. It is set low rather than high. At rest, the tail hangs in a slight curve like a saber. When the dog is excited or in motion, the curve is accentuated and the tail raised, but it should never be curled forward beyond a vertical line.

FOREQUARTERS:
The shoulder blades are long and obliquely angled, laid on flat and not placed forward. Both the upper arm and the shoulder blade are well muscled. The forelegs, viewed from all sides, are straight and the bone oval rather than round. The feet are short, compact with toes well arched, pads thick and firm, nails short and dark.

HINDQUARTERS:
The whole assembly of the thigh, viewed from the side, is broad, with both upper and lower thigh well muscled, forming as nearly as possible a right angle. The upper thigh bone parallels the shoulder blade while the lower thigh bone parallels the upper arm.

COAT:
The ideal dog has a double coat of medium length. The outer coat should be as dense as possible, hair straight, harsh and lying close to the body. A slightly wavy outer coat, often of wiry texture, is permissible. The head, including the inner ear and foreface, and the legs and paws are covered with short hair, and the neck with longer and thicker hair. The rear of the forelegs and hind legs has somewhat longer hair. The German Shepherd Dog varies in color, and most colors are permissible.

—Excerpts from the German Shepherd Dog Breed Standard

A good GSD owner absolutely must be able to interact with the dog in a self-confident manner. These dogs want their humans to be leaders; your dog will look to you for direction. It's important that you remain self-assured and fair with both corrections and praise. The German Shepherd is very independently minded. If you fail to instruct your dog in self-control or lack assertion, your dog will decide he can act on his own without permission. The breed's natural instinct is to protect and, if not trained properly, can result in the dog unexpectedly deciding a person is threatening and acting protectively. For these reasons, the GSD thrives best with a decisive owner who can think quickly and take firm control of his dog under all circumstances.

Once you bring a German Shepherd Dog into your home, take the time to train him properly. For training resources, including class information, search the AKC's extensive database for a training club in your area by visiting their site at www.akc.org/events/obedience/training_clubs. Successful training will lead to many happy years together with this happy, intelligent breed.

German Shepherds are friendly when in a relaxed setting. When well-trained, they get along great with children and other dogs.

At a Glance ...

The German Shepherd Dog is renowned throughout the world for his striking good looks and dutiful service to our society.

. . . .

The blueprint for the ideal GSD—the breed standard—is written and maintained by the breed's national parent club, the German Shepherd Dog Club of America, a member club of the American Kennel Club.

. . . .

German Shepherds were popular in Germany, where the breed originated, long before they arrived in the United States at the turn of the twentieth century.

. . . .

Highly active by nature, German Shepherds are great workers. Give yours plenty of time each day devoted to exercise and mental stimulation.

CHAPTER THREE

Shopping for a German Shepherd

Everyone who loves the German Shepherd Dog will want a perfect pet—one that is reliable, handsome, friendly, intelligent, and healthy. Once you've decided that the GSD is the dog for you, it's time to find a puppy. The American Kennel Club believes that there's only one source for a well-bred GSD puppy, and that is a responsible breeder. A puppy is only as good as his breeder, and investing time to find a breeder who produces healthy and stable GSD puppies is time well spent.

OFA A-OK

The Orthopedic Foundation for Animals (OFA) was founded by John M. Olin and a group of caring veterinarians and dog breeders in the mid-1960s. The goal of the foundation was to provide X-ray evaluations and guidance to dog breeders with regard to hip dysplasia, a common hereditary disease that affects many different breeds of dog.

Three OFA board-certified radiologists evaluate X-rays of dogs that are 24 months of age or older, scoring their hips as "Excellent," "Good," and "Fair," all of which are eligible for breeding. Dogs that score "Borderline," "Mild," "Moderate," and "Severe" should not be bred. The sire (father) and dam (mother) of your new puppy should have OFA numbers, proving that they passed a health screening test. For more information, visit www.offa.org.

Given the breed's many abilities and natural versatility, there may be more than one reason you want to add a GSD puppy to your home and family. Companionship and protection are the two most popular reasons that people opt for the German Shepherd. Few guardian breeds compare to the elegant and powerful GSD. Likewise, the breed excels as a show dog, obedience contender, agility competitor, farm dog, seeing eye dog, therapy dog, and just about any other task humans have found for canines. Whether you're looking for a pet for your children or a new dog to train in search and rescue, you will want to get a sound, healthy German Shepherd Dog with a good disposition. Only a good breeder can ensure that his puppy will make the grade. Why select a GSD if you're not going to get a dog that possesses correct breed characteristics, both physically and temperamentally?

A GOOD PUPPY IS WORTH THE WAIT

Slow down! If you're feeling seduced by the irresistible puppy faces on the pages of this book, that's perfectly normal. It's not, however, a good reason to race out and purchase the first furry, cute shepherd puppy you see. Good breeders tend to charge no more for a puppy than a lesser source, so do your homework before leaving home. And do yourself a favor: leave your checkbook and children at home when you make that first breeder visit.

PAPERWORK FOR PUREBREDS

The two most important papers for new dog owners are the pedigree and the registration form. The pedigree shows the puppy's family tree and should include the names of three to five generations of GSD ancestors. You likely will see titles in the pedigree, such as Ch. (Champion, a conformation prefix), CD (Companion Dog, an obedience title, used as a suffix), and HT (Herding Test, a herding trial title, used as a suffix). Each of these titles indicates an ancestor's accomplishments in some area of canine competition, which establishes the merits of the dogs in the puppy's background and reinforces the breeder's credibility. While we

German Shepherd Dogs and children can get along great. Just be sure to supervise all interactions between them.

Did You Know?

No breed's reputation suffered more greatly in America during the two World Wars than the German Shepherd Dog. Even though the breed's fame as a messenger and sentry dog for both the Axis and Allies during World War I was well known, the word "German" was omitted from the breed name in the United States and England. The temporary name "Alsatian" was used, and decades later, the simple term "Police Dog" was commonly heard.

know that a pedigree cannot guarantee health or good temperament, a well-constructed pedigree is still a virtual insurance policy and a good starting point. Registration papers indicate that the litter, sire (father), and dam (mother) are all registered with the AKC. If you have any intention of showing your German Shepherd Dog or participating in any other kind of AKC competitions, registration is essential. The breeder will provide you with individual registration forms to register your puppy. Usually the breeder will fill out parts of the form for you, but you will write in your name, address, puppy's name, and so forth. After submitting the registration forms and fee to the AKC, you will receive a Registration Certificate with your information on it, verifying that your puppy is included in the AKC database, and you are his new owner.

Shopping for a German Shepherd 31

When searching for a puppy, look for one that's well socialized and interacts well with his littermates, as well as people who come to visit them.

HOW TO FIND A PUPPY

You want a German Shepherd puppy but don't know where to start looking to find one? A good first step to finding the right puppy is to visit www.gsdca.org, the website of the German Shepherd Dog Club of America, the breed's parent club. Check out the breeder classifieds and the breeder and puppy ads. The listings are divided by area of the country, which is helpful and convenient for potential owners. Keep in mind: there are also many reputable German Shepherd breeders who are members of the GSDCA but do not advertise puppies on the site.

Contact the regional club affiliated with the GSDCA; the contact information can be found on the GSDCA website. There's no better source for firsthand information on German Shepherds in your area than the regional club. Another helpful resource is the AKC website, www.akc.org, which includes breeder referral listings and online breeder classifieds.

While it is entirely possible that a breeder in your area is selling sound, healthy pups, it's not recommended to consult a newspaper classified advertisement while looking for a puppy. Most breeders rely on referrals to sell their puppies, rather than advertising in the local paper. Be equally wary of online sellers of German Shepherds. Too often these websites belong to unscrupulous breeders or third-party sellers, who are solely interested in profit and turnaround—rather than in the well-being of the dogs that they are selling or the satisfaction of their customers.

Why Should you Register with the American Kennel Club?

Registering your new puppy with the American Kennel Club does more than just certify the lineage of your German Shepherd Dog. It helps the AKC do so many things for dogs everywhere, such as promoting responsible breeding and supporting the care and health of dogs throughout the world. As a result of your registration, the AKC is able to inspect kennels across the country, educate dog owners about the importance of training through the Canine Good Citizen® Program, support search and rescue canines via the AKC Companion Animal Recovery Canine Support and Relief Fund, teach the public about the importance of responsible dog ownership through our publications and annual AKC Responsible Dog Ownership Days, and much more. Not only is the AKC a respected organization dedicated to the registration of purebred dogs, but it is also devoted to the well-being of dogs everywhere. For more information, go to www.akc.org/reg.

QUESTIONS TO ASK THE BREEDER

Part of doing your homework is knowing the right questions to ask a breeder. Don't be shy or worry that the breeder will think you're a pest or a know-it-all. Good breeders are encouraged by potential owners who ask the right questions and show real interest in the welfare of the dogs that they're considering to buy.

It's important for new owners to know what answers to expect from good breeders:

1. Have you ever shown or competed with your German Shepherd Dogs in an AKC event (dog show, obedience trial, agility trial, or herding test)?

Experienced GSD breeders should be involved in some aspect of the dog fancy with their dog(s), perhaps showing in conformation or training them for some type of performance event or other dog-related activity. If you're considering a puppy for a particular kind of competition, such as conformation, herding trials, or agility, make sure to tell the breeder of your aspirations ahead of time, to help narrow down the selection.

2. How long have you been breeding GSDs? Do you raise other breeds? How many times do you breed your German Shepherds?

Most dog fanciers have been involved with their breed for a number of years prior to breeding their first litter. The more experience your breeder has in GSDs, the better your chances of getting a great puppy. It's possible that a new breeder will get lucky and produce a beautiful litter, but most bets are on the long-term breeder with a decade or two of experience in German Shepherds. Responsible breeders do not raise several different breeds of dogs or produce multiple litters of pups throughout the year. One or two litters a year is typical.

Rescue Me

If you do not have the time or patience to raise a puppy but still want a GSD, consider getting an adolescent or adult German Shepherd. The advantage of starting with an older dog is that his temperament and personality can be easily evaluated. One option is adopting a dog that needs re-homing. The German Shepherd Dog Club of America, the breed's parent club, has established the American German Shepherd Rescue Association, Inc., which assists local GSD clubs in establishing breed rescue groups. These groups take in unwanted GSDs, evaluate their health and personality, and then offer them for adoption to carefully screened homes. For more information, go to www.agsra.com.

Responsible Pet Ownership

Getting a dog is exciting, but it's also a huge responsibility. That's why it's important to educate yourself on all that is involved in being a good pet owner. As a part of the Canine Good Citizen® test, the AKC has a "Responsible Dog Owner's Pledge," which states:

I will be responsible for my dog's health needs.
- ☐ I will provide routine veterinary care, including check-ups and vaccines.
- ☐ I will offer adequate nutrition through proper diet and clean water at all times.
- ☐ I will give daily exercise and regularly bathe and groom.

I will be responsible for my dog's safety.
- ☐ I will properly control my dog by providing fencing where appropriate, by not letting my dog run loose, and by using a leash in public.
- ☐ I will ensure that my dog has some form of identification when appropriate (which may include collar tags, tattoos, or microchip identification).
- ☐ I will provide adequate supervision when my dog and children are together.

I will not allow my dog to infringe on the rights of others.
- ☐ I will not allow my dog to run loose in the neighborhood.
- ☐ I will not allow my dog to be a nuisance to others by barking while in the yard, in a hotel room, etc.
- ☐ I will pick up and properly dispose of my dog's waste in all public areas, such as on the grounds of hotels, on sidewalks, in parks, etc.
- ☐ I will pick up and properly dispose of my dog's waste in wilderness areas, on hiking trails, on campgrounds, and in off-leash parks.

I will be responsible for my dog's quality of life.
- ☐ I understand that basic training is beneficial to all dogs.
- ☐ I will give my dog attention and playtime.
- ☐ I understand that owning a dog is a commitment in time and caring.

3. Do you belong to the national club, the German Shepherd Dog Club of America, and any local or regional breed club?

Dedicated breeders often belong to the parent club or an area breed or kennel club. Such affiliation with other experienced fanciers and breeders expands their knowledge of shepherds.

4. Have you finished any champions or earned titles on any dogs?

Dog shows are meant to be a testing ground for breeders. Dogs that earn titles like "Champion" prove that they are superior stock and should be bred. The father and mother of the litter should be champions, and the breeder should proudly display photographs of victories in competition and any ribbons and trophies to prove his experience and success with and commitment to the breed.

5. What made you decide to breed these two dogs?

A conscientious breeder plans a litter of GSDs for specific reasons and should explain the genetics behind this particular breeding and what he expects it to produce. If the breeder tells you that the reason is simply that "my shepherd is sweet and/or beautiful and my neighbor's dog is handsome," he is a novice breeder. Passion and love for dogs alone does not qualify someone to be a good breeder.

6. Have you screened for all of the health concerns recommended by the German Shepherd Dog Club of America?

The breeder should have registered the sire (father) and dam's (mother) hips and elbows with the Orthopedic Foundation for Animals (OFA) because both hip and elbow dysplasia are found in the breed. OFA also keeps a registry

It's common for a pup's sire (father) to live off-site of the breeding facility, but the dam (mother) should be close by. She'll be a great indicator of the temperament and appearance that you can expect from your pup.

Look for a happy and healthy-looking puppy when visiting breeders. Pups reared in the home tend to be better socialized to people and the hustle and bustle of everyday life. But that's not to say that a kennel-reared puppy won't adapt easily, as well.

for osteochondritis dissecans (OCD), another joint disease to which the German Shepherd Dog is prone. Eye clearances are registered with the Canine Eye Registration Foundation (CERF). Visit the parent club's website for a complete list of health concerns in the breed.

7. Do you test the puppies' temperament?

Temperament tests are popular with many breeders. These are a series of simple tests that breeders use to gauge the temperament of different members of the litter. The GSDCA sponsors Temperament Test stations and provides guidelines for clubs sponsoring tests, which address behavior toward strangers, reaction to noise, visual stimuli, and footing.

8. May I meet the dam (mother) of the litter? And possibly the sire (father), if he lives on the property?

Temperament is just as hereditary as good looks! Seeing the puppy's dam and sire will give you a good idea of what your puppy could grow up to look like. It's possible that the sire is not on the premises, as many breeders purchase a stud service from a champion dog. Ask to see a photograph of the sire, and with any luck it will be a photo of him winning an award at a show or a trial. The dam, however, should be on the premises and appear healthy, vibrant, and friendly, despite the obvious burden of motherhood.

9. Have you raised the puppies in your home?

It should be instantly obvious that the breeder knows each pup individually. A breeder who's familiar with the litter will offer little details about each puppy and his personality. Puppies reared in a breeder's home often receive better socialization, but good breeders can raise wonderful, healthy, and happy puppies in a kennel as well.

10. **Do you have a standard sales contract, in addition to the registration papers and pedigree for me to review?**

Reputable breeders have sales contracts that include specific health guarantees and reasonable return policies. Your breeder should agree to accept a puppy back if things do not work out. The breeder also should be willing—indeed, anxious—to check up on the puppy's progress after he leaves and should be available if you have questions or problems.

VISITING THE BREEDER

Whether the breeder raises the puppies in his or her kitchen or in a separate kennel building on the property, you should be able to tell a lot about the breeder by surveying the surroundings. Don't be afraid to scrutinize the living area; it should be clean and orderly. There are advantages to a home-bred litter, certainly. The daily exposure to household noises, such as dishwashers, cell phones, televisions, and vacuum cleaners, makes the puppies' transition into pet life much easier. If the breeder is raising the pups in an outside kennel, that is perfectly fine, provided it's not a poorly kept garage or basement. Well-established breeders may have a separate outdoor facility for their adult dogs, with a special area for raising a litter or two. You'll know you've found a qualified breeder when the walls of the kennel (or kitchen) are lined with AKC champion certificates or ribbons from shows or trials.

The puppies should show no signs of lethargy, wariness, or compromised health. The pups themselves should be reasonably clean, bearing in mind that six-week-old GSD pups are poop-machines. Healthy puppies should appear energetic, bright-eyed and alert, and most of all friendly. If the breeder has done his job well, the puppies will be approachable and excited to see company. Socialization is a critical factor when bringing up puppies.

Healthy pups have clean, thick coats, are well proportioned, and feel solid and muscular without being overly fat and pot-bellied. Even though you will have a veterinarian check out the puppy after you purchase him, it's wise to watch for

Paper Goods

On the day that you pick up your puppy, the breeder should provide you with:

• **AKC papers to individually register your dog**

• **A pedigree for your dog (lists your puppy's family tree back at least five generations)**

• **Information about the pup's vaccinations and a recommended schedule to show your veterinarian**

• **Feeding advice, including information about which specific food the pup has been eating and how much**

• **A written sales agreement and guarantee, as well as certificates showing that the parents have been cleared by the OFA and CERF**

• **The breeder's contact information for any questions or concerns that might arise**

crusted eyes or noses and any watery discharge from the pup's nose, eyes, and ears. Be wary of any coughing or excessive sniffing or snorting. Check for evidence of watery or bloody stools. All of these may be signs of illness.

Perhaps the greatest advantage of purchasing a puppy from a breeder is that you have the opportunity to meet the dam (mother). Don't be surprised if the mom looks a bit weathered—you'd be disheveled too if you were rearing eight shepherd pups for eight weeks straight! It's not unusual for the dam to have a dull, thin coat or to be a bit underweight after weeks of nursing hungry pups.

By meeting the dam, you will get a pretty good idea of the personalities of the puppies. GSDs may be somewhat aloof with strangers, but they should not shy away from friendly overtures. It is normal for some dams to be protective of their litters, but she should never be overly aggressive with people. Good temperaments are inherited, just like good looks and strong protection and herding instincts.

Proper Paperwork

A responsible breeder will be able to provide your family with a pedigree and an American Kennel Club registration.

AKC Registration: When you buy a new GSD puppy from a breeder, ask the breeder for an American Kennel Club Dog Registration Application form. The breeder will fill out most of the application for you. When you fill out your portion of the document and mail it to the AKC, you will receive a Registration Certificate proving that your GSD is officially part of the AKC. Besides recording your name and your dog's name in the AKC database, registration helps fund canine health research, search-and-rescue teams, educating the public about responsible dog care, and much more.

Certified Pedigree: A pedigree is an AKC certificate proving that your dog is a purebred German Shepherd Dog. It is your puppy's family tree, showing the names of his parents and grandparents. If your dog is registered with the AKC, the organization will have a copy of your dog's pedigree on file, which you can order from its website (www.akc.org). Look for any titles that your GSD's ancestors have won, including any AKC dog shows, competitions, or certifications. A pedigree doesn't guarantee the health or good personality of a dog, but it's a starting point for picking out a good GSD puppy.

PINK OR BLUE?

Do you have your mind made up on a boy or a girl? You may instinctively feel like you know whether a male or a female is right for you. Certainly there are differences between the two, but both sexes are loving and protective, affectionate and loyal. Generally speaking, the differences are mainly due to individual personalities than to the sex of the animal. The adult male GSD is a larger dog, about 2 inches taller, and up to 20 pounds heavier than the female. For sheer size and power, the male will appear more imposing and impressive. The female, due to her heat cycles, can be a bit moody during her hormonal peaks if not spayed, though this varies greatly from female to female. The male can become dominant with strangers and other dogs, especially if not properly trained. Obedience lessons are highly recommended for all GSDs, if an owner expects the dog to regard him as the leader of the pack.

In female puppies, heat cycles can begin at six to nine months of age. In male puppies, both testicles should be descended into the scrotum by ten to twelve weeks of age. A dog with undescended testicles will not be eligible to compete in the show ring and should not be bred, but he nonetheless will make a fine pet. Intact males tend to be more territorial, especially around other male dogs. Neutering or spaying your male or female German Shepherd creates a level playing field and eliminates most of these sex-related differences, as well as minimizes or eliminates the threats of certain cancers.

BE CHOOSY

Above all else, do your homework and take your time while looking for the perfect pet. This isn't a race; it's a lifelong commitment. Make sure you understand exactly what type of dog you're bringing into your home. And evaluate whether you have the time, temperament, and home environment to dedicate to a German Shepherd Dog.

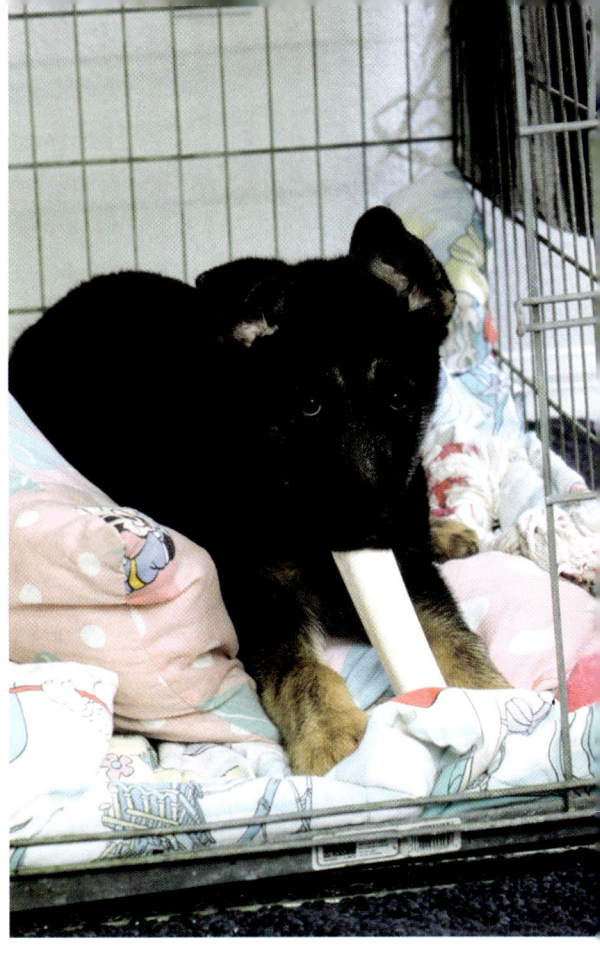

A good breeder will know his or her pups individually, sharing specific information on a particular puppy's personality. Heed the breeder's advice when deciding which puppy to take home.

At a Glance ...

Don't buy the first adorable German Shepherd that you see. It's worth the wait to find a happy, healthy puppy from a reputable breeder.

The breed's parent club, the German Shepherd Dog Club of America, is an excellent source for all things GSD. Endorsed by the American Kennel Club, the GSDCA governs the breed's standard and facilitates events around the United States.

Be prepared with a list of questions to ask each breeder when looking for a potential pup. Likewise, be ready to answer questions about yourself and pet-owning experience, as well.

When visiting breeders, keep an eye out for clean, hospitable facilities and well-socialized puppies and dams. You'll want to find a pup that's been reared to be friendly and trusting of people.

CHAPTER FOUR

Your Dog's New Home

When your new GSD puppy comes home, he will most likely be eight to ten weeks old, the age that most breeders will release a puppy to his new home. Before you collect your new charge, make sure you have the essentials at home, and prepare your home much like you would for a toddler. Puppy-proofing the home is similar to baby-proofing: you have to consider how your home and yard appear from your puppy's

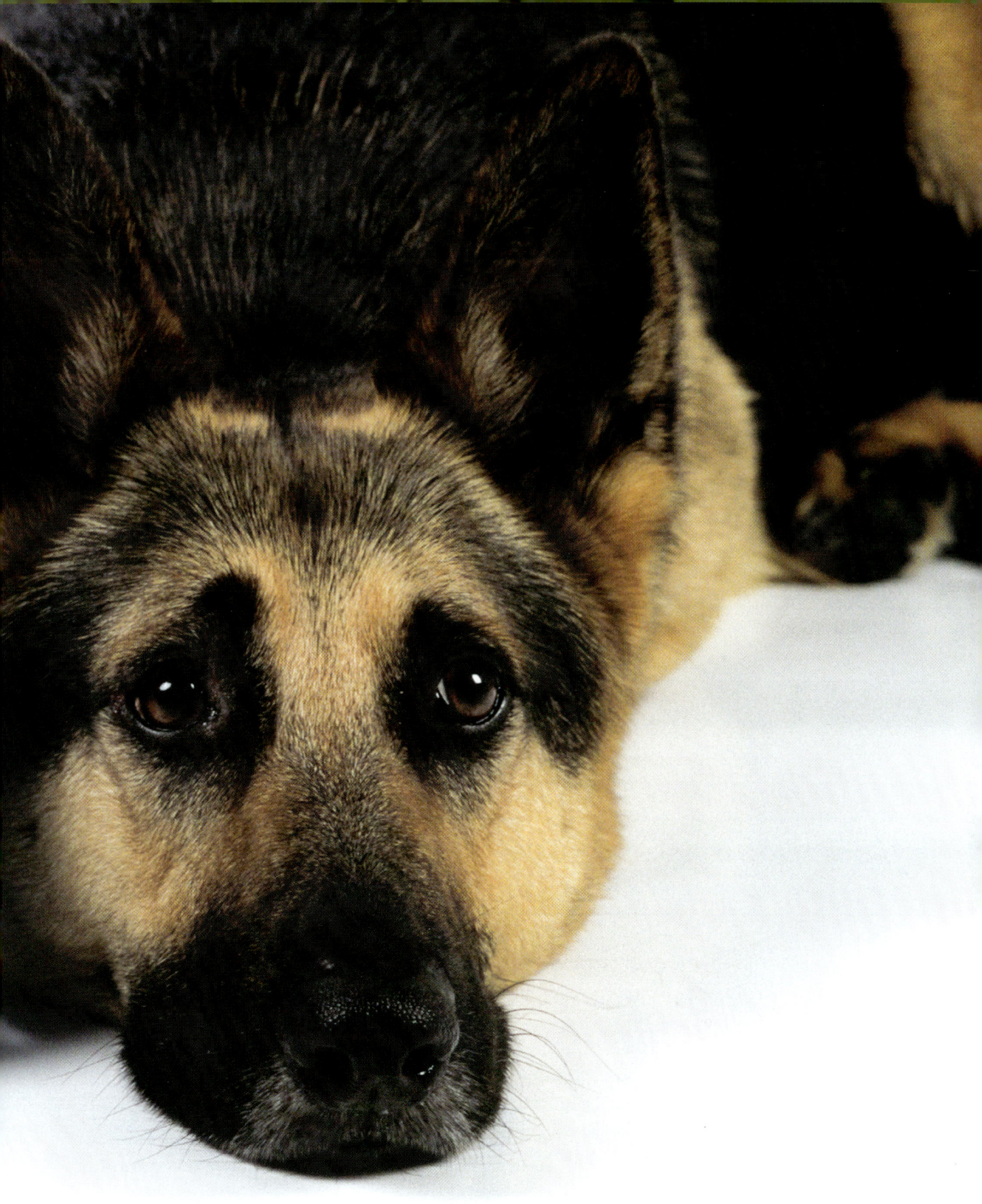

perspective, which means you have to get down on all fours. Puppies, like babies, enjoy putting things in their mouths, eating anything in their paths, and wreaking joyous havoc in the home. It's your job as owner and pet parent to keep your young one safe and to protect your possessions from destruction.

SHOPPING FOR PUPPY'S NEEDS

Before your puppy comes home, be sure to go shopping. Pet-supply stores offer an array of more products than you or your puppy can imagine. To begin, let's make sure you have the essentials.

Food: If you ask your puppy, he'll say that the most important thing to purchase is f-o-o-d! In this case, your puppy is right. Choose a quality dog food for your puppy, following the advice of the puppy's breeder. It's best to continue feeding what the breeder selected, especially if the puppy eats it with gusto.

The manufacturers of quality dog food offer special formulas for different size dogs, sometimes even breed-specific, and for various life stages. A large-breed puppy formula will satisfy all of your German Shepherd Dog's nutritional requirements for the first year of life. Feeding a fast-growing dog like a GSD demands that you purchase a balanced, complete food that will encourage proper development of bones, muscle, and body. Beyond the first year of age, an adult-maintenance formula designed for large breeds is recommended. Never skimp on the quality of a puppy's food. It is true that quality food from a pet-supply store will cost more than some commercial brands that are sold in supermarkets, but the long-lasting effects of good food on your puppy are well worth the investment. Responsible dog owners and breeders never compromise on the quality of the food they provide.

Food Bowls: Purchase two bowls. You can decide whether or not you want the standard stainless steel bowls or perhaps something fancier and fun. Ceramic or plastic bowls look nice and can be more personal, such as a flower-lined pink bowl for a girl puppy or a bone-lined blue bowl for a boy. But beware that some dogs can be allergic to plastic and will require ceramic or stainless steel instead. Practically speaking, stainless steel will last the longest and can be sterilized in the dishwasher. GSD pups love to chew, so a hard plastic bowl can unintentionally become a chew toy, which is not a good thing. Get a tip-proof bowl to prevent your GSD pup from playing and splashing in his water bowl.

Leash and Collar: It's best to start your growing puppy in an adjustable collar, one that will expand as his neck widens. Adjustable collars can be made of nylon or leather. For puppies, a lightweight nylon collar is preferred. Your GSD pup's first leash should be a narrow 6-foot nylon or cloth leash, which will work well on daily walks and for puppy kindergarten classes. Once your dog gets older, you can switch to a leather collar and leash ensemble.

When shopping for a crate, look for one that will fit your pup when he becomes fully grown.

A traditional identification tag attached to the puppy's collar should include your name, address, and phone number on the tag. In this age of Global Positioning System technology, it's no surprise that some dog collars come equipped with these gizmos. You can purchase a high-tech dog collar with a built-in GPS that will alert you (via phone or email) whenever you German Shepherd wanders away from his designated area.

A second leash that's worth exploring is the flexible lead, which is a 12- or 16-foot nylon cord housed in the handle that extends by using a button. Once the puppy has learned to walk on a traditional lead, utilizing a flexible lead makes exercising the puppy more enjoyable and much easier.

Sleeping Quarters: Two items are essentials for the GSD puppy: a simple, soft dog bed and a wire crate. Visiting a pet-supply center or pet shop, you'll see

Keep Toys New

Only offer two or three toys to your puppy at a time. If you give your German Shepherd too many toys, he'll get bored with all of them and get into trouble around the house. Only give him a few toys at a time and rotate them often. Each week, he will be excited to play with something new!

a large selection of dog beds—some of which are fancy and elegant, and others functional and basic. For a puppy who's all teeth with little control over his bladder, the simple bed makes more sense. Choose a bed that launders easily so that you can handle accidents promptly and without fuss.

You'll also see a variety of dog crates in the pet store. The ideal crate for a German Shepherd Dog is a wire crate that measures about 24 to 26 inches wide and 30 inches high, so that it can be used by the adult GSD as well. The crate provides your puppy with a secure den and the required structure for house-training.

Comb and Brush: Shepherd puppies have a lot of fur, so start brushing your pup's coat as soon as he comes home. A basic soft bristle brush will do the job, removing any dead hair and stimulating the coat oils. It's important that your puppy gets used to his coat being brushed from an early age. Once your puppy is a few months old, a slicker brush (containing small metal pins in a rubber base), a steel comb (with wide-spaced and narrowly spaced teeth), a mat rake, and a shedding comb will be on your grooming shopping list. You can also purchase a quality shampoo made specially for dogs once your puppy is a few months old.

Toys: The pet-supply store is practically a toy store for puppies! You'll find aisles of fun and enticing dog toys made of rubber, nylon, rawhide, plastic, cloth, and more. Purchase a soft toy and a hard toy, perhaps a stuffed animal-type toy with a squeaker inside and a medium-sized rawhide bone. A rubber ball will never go to waste in a GSD puppy's home. Most importantly, purchase safe toys and don't overdo it all at once. Just remember: a puppy with a dozen toys is no happier than a puppy with two or three—as long as he has his owner nearby to engage him.

BRINGING PUPPY HOME

Being thrust into an unknown environment without the furry support of his littermates and the people he knows is very stressful for any puppy. There are many ways to make this transition less traumatic.

Whether you are picking up your puppy from the breeder or from the airport, arrange to have someone accompany you to comfort the puppy. Use the car's seatbelt to secure a puppy-size crate. If you will be alone, put the crate in the passenger seat and face the crate door toward you so the puppy can see you and so you can stick your fingers through the mesh to let the puppy smell you. This way he can see your face when you speak to him. If the puppy is not accustomed to being crated, it is much easier to put him in rear-first, so he can't resist by using his front paws. Your puppy will be able to relax more in the crate—at least after his initial protests at being caged. Do not let the puppy loose in the car; it's dangerous and can be deadly in a car accident. Use a large towel or other soft material to wrap the puppy so he has something to snuggle into. Physical contact of some sort is a very important stress reliever in all dogs—but especially so for a puppy that is used to having his mother and littermates close by.

Puppy-Proof for Peace of Mind

New puppy owners needn't worry about their puppies getting into mischief and potentially harming themselves, as long as they do a full house sweep prior to the puppy coming home.

Your GSD pup will get into anything that you leave lying out. So be sure to store trash cans, cleaning supplies, and any other dangerous materials out of his reach.

■ In the bathroom, raise the trash can from the floor. Be sure the puppy can't reach medicine bottles, dental floss, toilet bowl cleaners, and any other chemical items.

■ In the bedroom and throughout the house, unplug any electrical cords and pick up your personal garments (under clothes, socks, etc.). Keep ashtrays away from puppies, as well.

■ In the kitchen, hide cleaning supplies (including mops and buckets) and secure electrical cords (unplug any that aren't needed). Secure kitchen cabinets with safety stoppers. Keep the kitchen garbage away from the puppy's nose and paws.

■ The garage (or shed) is potentially the worst area for a puppy. Place roach and rodent poisons and antifreeze out of reach. Keep fertilizers and other chemical agents out of the puppy's reach, as well.

Let your new GSD pup slowly explore his new home. He'll have a lot to adjust to all at once, so be patient and try to make each new situation calm and fun.

HOME INTRODUCTION

When you first bring home your GSD puppy, do your best to keep every experience and interaction calm, peaceful, and fun. It will help him acclimate to his new home more easily and without anxiety.

WELCOME WAGON

Keep the number of people in the yard and home for your puppy's first introduction limited to just one or two besides you. First thing, when you get home, take your German Shepherd immediately to the place where he will be expected to eliminate. Just set the puppy down and let him start to explore at his own pace while you follow close by, speaking comfortingly to him and offering him gentle touches if he seems hesitant. After a few minutes, if he has a dire need to eliminate, he will do so. Treat and praise your puppy, then take him in the house to quietly explore for a few more minutes. Stay right by your puppy, and pick him up and take him back out to the yard if he starts to wander or circle with his nose to the floor. It's a telltale sign that he needs to go again. Be patient; chances are his urge to go will fade for a few minutes, as soon as you pick him up to move him. Keep an eye on your puppy whenever he isn't confined to his pen or crate, and be patient and reward correct behavior when he eliminates in the correct place. These are the keys to successful house-training.

A PIECE OF HISTORY

Starting with World War I, and in every major war since then, German Shepherd Dogs have proven themselves as valiant soldiers and have saved the lives of many thousands of men. Some of the duties they have performed are: mercy dogs (locating wounded men on the battlefield, and guiding help to them or attempting to pull them to safety), messenger dogs (carrying medical or other supplies during battles), sentry dogs, mine detectors, scout dogs (locating hidden enemies and booby traps), and guard dogs. A bronze German Shepherd statue at a pet cemetery in Hartsdale, New York, serves as a monument to WWI dogs. An annual Memorial Day ceremony is conducted there to honor all military dogs.

After your puppy is finished with his initial exploration and elimination, offer him his usual food. Then it is time to rest, so your puppy can relax from the stress of all this newness. Put him in his crate, pen, or wherever you decide his personal space will be, and leave him with a few items to make him feel at home, such as a soft stuffed toy or rolled-up towels to simulate his littermates, a dish of water he cannot tip over, and whatever food he didn't eat earlier. Your puppy may fuss for a few minutes; if you want to keep him company, sit or lie quietly nearby, but don't take him out of his rest area until he is quiet. If you want to respond to his whining by speaking softly to reassure him in a monotone voice that he is not alone, that's fine; but using sweet "puppy talk" to comfort him would be rewarding the undesired behavior of fussing when being put to bed—a bad habit that you don't want to encourage.

Your puppy should soon fall asleep. Check back frequently to see if he is awake and let him out as soon as he is; don't wait until he's crying and fussing. If your German Shepherd pup does start to fuss, wait until there is a pause in the behavior and then quickly let him out. Letting him out while he is being noisy only reinforces the behavior.

NIGHTY NIGHT

The first night in his new home will be difficult for your puppy. Place his crate or pen near your bed, so you can hear the pup if he fusses; then you'll easily be able to comfort him so that he realizes he's not alone. Consider keeping a night light on in the room to help reduce any puppy anxiety.

German Shepherds crave stability. Provide yours with a structured home life, and he will quickly settle in to the routine.

Small Dangers

Some less obvious items that can hurt your puppy are dental floss, yarn, needles and thread, and other stringy stuff. Puppies exploring the house at ground level will find and swallow the tiniest of objects and can end up in surgery. Veterinarians have far too many stories they could share about the strange items they have removed from puppies' tummies.

You'll undoubtedly have to make potty trips throughout the night, while house-training your young pup. If he seems restless, such as pacing or circling, take him to the elimination location and wait for him to do his business. This means you need to keep shoes and a jacket handy, as puppies usually do not start showing signs that they need to go until immediately prior to their physiological maximum control of elimination. Just as with newborn babies, puppies need to eliminate once or more during the night, so be prepared for your sleep to be interrupted for at least a few weeks.

CHILD INTERACTION

If there are children in your family, instruct them on proper behavior around the puppy before he arrives. This includes using the correct method to introduce themselves to the puppy, speaking in soft voices, and using slow movements around the puppy for a few days. Younger children should be instructed to never pick up the puppy because accidentally dropping him can injure the dog, both physically and emotionally, by making it harder for the pup to learn to trust handling. Instead, have children sit on the floor and hold the German Shepherd puppy in their lap. Explain to younger children that the puppy is like a baby that needs to sleep often so he can grow healthily. Teach your children never to disturb the puppy if he is sleeping. There are several excellent books available on raising children and dogs together that can provide successful methods of coping and point out potential problems to be avoided.

SHEPHERD SOCIALIZATION

The road to socialization is paved with puppy love. The most essential ingredient in a well-behaved, happy puppy is trust in his surroundings, both human and physical. GSD puppies from breeders have the distinct advantage of socialization—that is, daily human contact. By nature, GSDs are protective working dogs that bond to a single person or family; they are selective about which people they choose to have around them and trust. When not exposed to people—both adults and children—at a young age, the puppy can grow up to be insecure and even fearful. Breeders who raise their puppies in their homes do the puppy one better—exposure to an indoor home environment, complete with strange sounds (door bells, dishwashers, vacuum cleaners, television, etc.).

Sadly, many behavioral issues arise because puppies were not actively socialized during their youth. Growling, barking, fear-biting, and other aggressive behaviors can be avoided if the puppy is introduced to different people, other dogs, and new

environments on a regular basis. Aggression and other behavior problems can be difficult to eliminate in a grown dog, but they don't ever have to begin. Socialization and early training are the building blocks to a happy, well-behaved adult German Shepherd Dog.

The first twenty weeks of a puppy's life are the most critical period in socialization. Breeders typically release puppies from their dams (mothers) at eight

Make new introductions slowly. Treats are a great tool to aid in the process. Wait until your puppy is comfortable in your home before introducing him to the neighbors.

Consider the Microchip

In addition to a dog collar, you should think about having your vet or breeder insert a microchip in your dog to help find him if he ever gets lost. The microchip, when scanned, will show your dog's unique microchip number so that your German Shepherd Dog can be returned to you as soon as possible. Since 1995, the American Kennel Club has offered the Companion Animal Recovery (AKC CAR) program to responsible pet owners, and this 24/7 recovery service has been selected by millions of dog owners who are grateful for the peace of mind and service that AKC CAR offers. Learn more at www.akccar.org.

Your Dog's New Home **49**

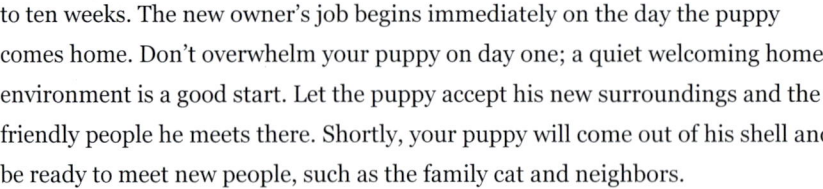

From the Ground Up

The best way to puppy-proof any room is to get down on all fours; that way, you see the room from your GSD puppy's perspective. You never know what dangerous things you might find this way. For example, a stray rubber band or a half-eaten candy bar hidden under the couch. These things can be very dangerous, so make sure to "crawl" around to complete your puppy-proofing sweep of the house.

to ten weeks. The new owner's job begins immediately on the day the puppy comes home. Don't overwhelm your puppy on day one; a quiet welcoming home environment is a good start. Let the puppy accept his new surroundings and the friendly people he meets there. Shortly, your puppy will come out of his shell and be ready to meet new people, such as the family cat and neighbors.

HUMAN INTRODUCTIONS

Be certain to have your puppy meet children: frequent interaction with young people leaves a lasting impression on an adult GSD's temperament. Meeting children brings out the breed's natural protective nature—in other words, the best in the German Shepherd. Whenever your puppy meets children, make sure to supervise the encounter. Shepherds may attempt to dominate little people, treating them almost like littermates, and they become protective of the kids. As herding dogs, German Shepherds also may attempt to pen toddlers, nipping at their feet or corralling them with the head. This type of behavior can scare children and overwhelm them. Some children may be more assertive and tease, grab at, and hurt the puppy. Always be on the ready to come to the aid of both child and pup. Children should be instructed not to taunt or jump on a puppy or to instigate bad behavior in the puppy.

A romp through the neighborhood, a visit to the dog park, the beach, any outdoor event all make ideal opportunities for the puppy to experience a slice of human life. Make a point of going on a couple of weekly outings where the puppy will encounter lots of different people and activity. Always keep the experiences positive for the puppy. It's not productive for him to have scary, bad experiences, so you must be in control of the situation and remove the puppy from any experience that becomes overwhelming. For instance, if your puppy is a little panicked by a passing motorcycle, a noisy construction site, or fireworks, be kind and remove him from the scary chaos. In due time, he'll be better able to deal with strange circumstances.

CANINE INTRODUCTIONS

A puppy class is also an excellent forum to continue your pup's socialization. Puppy classes accept puppies as young as ten to twelve weeks of age and concentrate on basic manners, encouraging puppies to trust and respect their owners. The amount of time an owner spends with his puppy prior to twenty weeks of age pays huge dividends in the adult dog—quality time spent during the first few months of ownership yields a more obedient, biddable, and respectful adult dog. Puppy classes may also introduce your GSD to simple games that you can later use to transition into training commands. Interaction and fun are the main components of puppy classes, and your pup should get the idea that structured fun time with his owner can lead to good things. Obedience classes are just around the corner.

If puppy classes are not an option and you want to find opportunities for your German Shepherd to meet other dogs, try to arrange visits with other puppies and calm puppy-friendly dogs owned by your neighbors or friends. Hold your puppy in your hands on the ground or floor until he has met the strange dog

and they have sniffed each other, face and rear. If the other dog is also a puppy, he should be held by a second person. If it's an adult dog, ask him to sit or down stay until your puppy gains confidence and voluntarily approaches the other dog. If there is more than one dog for your pup to meet, introduce them all individually. Expect an older dog to growl at an over-exuberant puppy, sometimes even to put his mouth over the puppy. As long as the older dog is calm and deliberate, and not completely rejecting the puppy, allow this behavior; the older dog is teaching the puppy "dog manners" (acceptable inter-dog behaviors) which he cannot learn from humans. The puppy may cringe but should quickly re-approach the older dog, who should accept some calmer puppy behaviors such as play biting and pawing without disciplining the puppy.

A social puppy is a happy puppy. Once he's settled in, enroll your pup in a class to learn to properly socialize with others.

At a Glance ...

Before you bring your puppy home, stock up on all the essential items you'll need to care for your new German Shepherd Dog, including food, bedding, a crate or pet gates, toys, and treats.

First things first, show your puppy exactly where to go to the bathroom the moment you bring him home.

Start off right, and have your GSD pup sleep in his crate from the first night you bring him home. Keep him in the room with you, if having him nearby will make you both feel better.

Supervise all interactions between your German Shepherd and children. Though well-intentioned in their playtime, both can easily get hurt.

Begin your puppy's socialization process as soon as he's old enough to go outdoors and interact with new people and dogs in various settings.

CHAPTER FIVE

School Days

Every GSD puppy has enormous potential to learn. Few breeds have the reputation that the German Shepherd Dog has to become a true superdog.

The world has witnessed this breed excel in countless capacities—from working farm dogs and guard dogs, to police and military dogs, to search-and-rescue dogs, to Hollywood movie stunt dogs, to obedience trial champions and top-winning show dogs. Just imagine all that

It's important to start your puppy's behavior training early, but be sure to also give him plenty of time to just play and be a puppy.

potential residing in that little eight-week-old ball of fur who's chewing on your sneaker!

It's a huge responsibility for the owner of such a remarkable animal, but your German Shepherd Dog can be all he can be as long as you're ready to train him, stimulate his mind, and provide the leadership he needs. Puppies want to know who's the boss and to understand what's expected of them—that's key to their nature as pack animals.

Obedience training is the way to develop a dog that you can trust with your life, with your children and family, in your home and yard, and around other dogs and people in the community. Such a powerful, protective dog needs to be controlled, and his energies and talents must be channeled in positive ways. His first leader, of course, was his dam (mother), who laid down the rules and corrected him when he erred. You, as his owner, become his next leader and the most important person in his life.

POSITIVE REINFORCEMENT

An important difference between the dam's approach to teaching and yours is that the dam did not read a chapter in a dog training book and learn that positive reinforcement works better than mouthing a puppy by the neck and shaking him. A basic precept of canine behavioral science is the idea that a rewarded behavior is always repeated. That means that if you give your puppy a pat on the head and a cookie when he does something good, like peeing outside or sitting on command, he will do it again for the sake of a treat. Some owners like to think that the dog is doing it for both the cookie and for love, but it's definitely about the treat. Any owner who rewards undesirable behaviors in the same way, such as giving the dog a treat for jumping up or for barking senselessly, will do his hapless part in nurturing a dog with bad habits.

Positive reinforcement does not mean that you say "yes, yes, YES" every time your dog does something good or bad. You can still tell a dog "no" without ruining him for life. It is far better to give a dog a simple correction than to deal with bad behavior. Dogs respect authority: the puppy did not resent his mother for shaking him and growling. Puppies get the message and shape up when their mothers say so (or else they get stepped on and snarled at—which is never fun).

Of course, close supervision of your puppy helps make his education easier. No matter how carefully you puppy-proof your living space, your GSD puppy will find something to get into. You can't hide every pillow, shoe, and curtain tassel from your pup. When you catch him snooping in the garbage can (or a grocery bag or your purse), simply remove him from the object (or move the object from him) and tell him "no." You can't teach your puppy right from wrong with just kisses and chicken! Save those treats for rewarding good behavior, and your puppy will learn that his alpha pack leader (you!) only gives him the good stuff when he behaves properly.

When training our dogs, we tend to mistakenly assume that our dogs speak English and intuitively understand human standards of life. It makes no sense to a puppy that you sit at a table and consume super-fragrant food while he has to stay locked in his crate. By canine standards, that's inappropriate and rude: the whole pack (family) should stand around and watch the alpha eat; then all the underlings dive in when the alpha is done eating. Canine meals naturally are accompanied by lots of growling, posturing, and flying food and fur. Human mealtime standards (in most homes) don't resemble that. Make your intentions clear to your puppy. At dinnertime, you can put him in his crate and give him a cookie for settling down. Then serve your pot roast and ignore your puppy. The message is clear: alpha is eating, and you are to remain quiet until you're released. Rewarding the puppy for being quiet in his crate after your meal will reinforce his good behavior.

Did You Know?

Dogs do not like to be patted on the head any more than people do. Dogs feel insecure when a stranger bends over and reaches toward the top of their head. Many dogs have been labeled "shy" because they back away when someone does this to them. The proper way to greet any unfamiliar dog is to bend at the knees or sit in a chair so you are near the dog's level, then hold out a hand for the dog to approach and sniff while speaking softly. If the dog is relaxed, perhaps shown by wagging his tail below the level of his back, and makes eye contact without staring after he smells your hand, then you can rub his chest and behind his ears, and then stroke down his back. This greeting encourages trust.

School Days 55

German Shepherd Dogs have the potential to understand hundreds of words—both commands (like *sit, stay, heel, up,* etc.) and phrases (like "Good girl," "Ready for a walk?" and "Are you hungry?"). Dogs associate behaviors and activities with certain words. If you ever have the opportunity to watch a dog running through an agility course, you will be astonished by how much English the dog appears to understand. A handler can say, "Start over," "Weave poles next," "Go slowly on this one," and the dog instantly and intuitively responds. We know that dogs are capable of understanding far more words than just "sit," "stay," and "stop-that-barking."

Dogs exist in the "here and now"—we know they don't go to sleep at night and worry about who's going to take them out tomorrow or how they'll do at the big dog show in the morning. The future is not part of a dog's mental makeup, which is actually a nice way to live if you can. Likewise, a dog doesn't dwell on past mistakes or regrets, though dogs do have a memory for past events and people they've met. When training your GSD, keep in mind that the dog lives in

No Biting

It's essential to teach your puppy to use his mouth softly when interacting with people. Puppy teeth are needle sharp, and they are used to biting their littermates who have protective fur and loose skin. Puppies need to be taught to use less force with people. Some trainers suggest never letting your puppy or adult dog put his mouth on you, in the mistaken idea that this will promote aggressive biting later. In fact, teaching your puppy how to modulate his bite for humans' extremely tender skin serves to prevent accidental bites. Often, dogs that have been allowed to mouth and explore human hands and arms, learning self-control, will later be able to give non-damaging play bites and "warning" bites to those (especially children) who have violated the rules of proper social conduct.

The method is very simple: When the puppy's teeth start to hurt, do what another dog would do—yelp loudly and withdraw your body part and attention from the puppy for a second or two, until he glances into your face to see if you are willing to continue the game. Then let the puppy resume, saying "OK," which will become your verbal cue when something is an approved behavior. Repeat as many times as it takes for your puppy to restrain his bite, then immediately praise him when he bites gently. The contrast between the intrinsic satisfaction (reward) of mouthing and social interaction, coupled with the negative (undesired by the puppy) loud noise and social withdrawal of his favorite person will quickly teach the puppy to control his mouth.

Don't assume that your GSD knows English. Both you and your dog need to learn the meaning of each others' body language in order to train successfully.

Expend the Energy

Puppies need a regular regimen of exercise and play so they can relax during calm periods of self-play or rest. An overabundance of energy and lack of acceptable activities to engage their interest may lead to puppy fussiness and chewing. Provide enough exercise, interactive play, and training to settle the dog before you leave him alone or unsupervised; it will greatly increase the chance that your puppy will stay calm during his down time.

the moment and that only the things happening right now matter to him. If you come home and find that your puppy has uprooted a philodendron from its planter and spread dirt on your carpet, reprimanding him for his bad gardening skills will not mean a thing to him. He will likely believe that you don't care for that sour-tasting house plant either. However, if you happen to catch the puppy shaking the philodendron in his mouth and shout "no!" then your puppy will instantly understand that what he's doing is unacceptable. Dogs must be caught in the act in order to accept blame—you have to witness it in order to prosecute; no amount of physical evidence will convince a dog that he's guilty of the crime you discover. Timing and consistency are critical to your ability to train your dog and teach him right from wrong.

TEN KEYS TO SUCCESSFUL TRAINING

1. Trust is essential for the relationship between you and your dog. A dog's desire to please you and obey you sprouts from his trust in you. Never betray your dog by making him think that you cannot be trusted 24/7.

2. Keep it simple and monosyllabic. Use one-word and one-syllable commands to teach basic behaviors (sit, down, come).

3. Give the command once and use authority in your voice. If you repeat the command four times, the puppy may wait for the fifth time to see if you *really* mean it.

4. Praise the puppy for good behavior. Treats, kisses, and pats translate into dog as "job well done."

5. Consistency is next to dogliness! What's acceptable on Monday must be okay on Tuesday and Wednesday. You can't allow the dog to jump up on the bed on Monday, when you're in a good mood or have time to spare, and then scold the dog for the same behavior two days later. A confused dog will soon become a lovable, but untrained and undisciplined monster.

6. Catch the puppy in the act. Correcting the puppy for something he did an hour ago is meaningless to the dog and frustrating for you. Clean up the mess and be more vigilant next time.

7. Hands off! Physical corrections have no place in dog training. Smacking a dog with a rolled-up newspaper only proves to the dog that you are untrustworthy. Hitting the dog in any manner sends the same bad message to the dog.

8. Tone is more important than words. When you want your dog to obey, don't use your happy "good dog" voice. Be authoritative and firm, and the dog will know you mean business. Save the happy voice for giving treats and praise.

9. "Come," they told me. The recall is the most important command to teach a dog. Recall means the dog comes to you when called. Always praise your dog for coming to you. You want him to know that he will get a treat and a kiss every time he comes to you. Never call your dog to you so that you can scold him for a behavior (which he no longer remembers).

10. Dogs understand structure. Creatures of habit by nature, canines respond best to a set routine so that they can anticipate what's coming. Mealtimes, short training sessions, walks, playtimes, socialization sessions, and so forth are the structure dogs look for. Structure can lead to good behavior and consistency.

Make your Puppy a S.T.A.R.

New puppy owners should investigate the American Kennel Club's newest training program for puppies called AKC S.T.A.R. Puppy. Learning to communicate with your puppy can happen even better in an organized training class, and the puppy training classes provide great opportunities for your dog to interact with other young pups. The instructor in a puppy training class should be a qualified professional able to answer questions about everything from house-training and problem behaviors to how to get involved in obedience trials. Owners can learn firsthand the best ways to teach certain commands and practical skills.

What makes your puppy a S.T.A.R.? Socialization, Training, Activity, and Responsibility spell success in these classes. Once you and your puppy have completed a basic six-week training course, you can be tested by a S.T.A.R. evaluator on everything you've learned. Once you pass the test, you can send the application to the AKC and be enrolled in the S.T.A.R. Puppy Program and receive a certificate and medallion. Visit www.akc.org/starpuppy for details.

Dogs don't have the added benefit of positive-reinforcement training when interacting with each other. Whereas they will rely on nipping, growling, and yelping to convey their displeasure, you have a host of tools at your disposal—such as treats, praise, and physical contact.

Read Up

Citizen Canine: Ten Essential Skills Every Well-Mannered Dog Should Know (BowTie Press, 2010) is the only official training publication by the American Kennel Club about the CGC Program. The book, written by Mary R. Burch, the director of the program, is a training primer for owners to pass the CGC test with flying colors. A chapter is devoted to each of the ten CGC tests, plus there's information or activities that dogs and owners can pursue beyond the CGC. The book is available directly from the American Kennel Club or from any quality book retailer.

KINDERGARTEN PLAYTIME

Every GSD puppy likes fun and food, and puppy games are all about both. Some games are just that, entertainment and play, while others can lay the foundation for obedience commands further down the road.

"Catch Me If You Can" is a favorite game for every herding breed. Your puppy can follow you around the yard, as you turn to him and clap and call his name. He's learning his name and getting to know you for the fun, trustworthy human you are.

If you have a friend to join you, play a variation on this called **"Come, Shepherd, Come."** Hold the puppy in your arms and have your friend sit a few yards away. Place the puppy on the floor between you while your friend calls him, using the pup's name sandwiched by the word "come." When the puppy runs to your friend, have him lavish praise and a treat on your GSD. Then it's your turn to call the puppy, giving him praise but no treat. You and your friend can alternate giving praise, treats, or both.

"Retrieve" is a game that shepherds love almost as much as Labrador and Golden Retrievers! Just add a tennis ball to the "Come, Shepherd, Come" game—just toss the ball from side to side and reward the puppy for retrieving the ball and releasing it to the person.

"Find Your Toy" teaches the puppy the names of his various toys and encourages him to use his nose and eyes to search for things. Place the puppy's favorite squeaky toy in the middle of the room and say, "Find your baby (or frog

Be a Good Citizen

The AKC's Canine Good Citizen® Program stresses responsible ownership and good manners for dogs. The test itself involves ten steps that ensure that the dog is a well-trained, mannerly citizen of the community. All ten exercises are performed with a dog in a buckle collar attached to a leash. After basic puppy training classes and the AKC S.T.A.R. Puppy Program, the CGC® test is the next step toward training dogs. The owners of more than half a million dogs that have earned the CGC designation since the program began in 1989 recognize that there is true benefit and joy in training a dog. Many of these owners have gone on to explore obedience and agility trials, dog shows, tracking, and other performance events with their dogs. The CGC test is administered by certified evaluators at dog training schools, dog shows, and AKC Responsible Dog Ownership Days across the country. Find out more at www.akc.org/events/cgc/Index.cfm.

or squirrel)" and reward him for finding it. After doing this several times, place the toy a little farther away, with only part of the toy in plain sight. Tell him to find his toy, then let him go search for it. This time when he finds it, give him more elaborate praise and a treat.

"**Roughhouse**" is every dog's favorite rough-and-tumble game. GSDs love when their owners get a little silly and engage them in a playful round of wrestling. Get down on all fours and slap the floor while calling your dog's name. Puppies go wild when they see their owners in play mode. This game proves to the puppy that you're trustworthy in every situation and demonstrates how much physical contact he can use when playing. Always set limits for your puppy when roughhousing: you don't want the game to get out of control with biting and tugging. Never allow children to engage in this kind of play.

"**Tug of War**" with a nylon rope toy can be great fun for a puppy. The key to this game is to let your puppy win some of the time. This builds confidence in your puppy. No game should frustrate the puppy because he never can win.

"**Hide-and-Seek**" can also be used to lay the groundwork for good recall. You can play this game indoors or outdoors, hiding behind a sofa or a tree when the puppy is not looking. Peek out just far enough so that the puppy can see you and call his name. Puppies love the notion that their human is being naughty or silly and will come running to investigate what mischief you're into. Call out "Come to me" as the puppy is running toward you. Give him lots of praise when he reaches you. Any game that reinforces the puppy's trust and confidence in you is time well spent. German Shepherd Dogs are naturally suspicious dogs, so proving to them over and over that you are trustworthy is a good thing.

Instill trust in your GSD pup early, and he will grow to become a truly valuable companion for life.

At a Glance ...

German Shepherd Dogs are highly trainable canines. For years, they've been the go-to dogs for service and assistance work, as well as many Hollywood films.

Obedience training will help mold your unruly GSD puppy into a well-mannered, helpful member of your home.

Start early and stay consistent in your training. Otherwise, your puppy will be confused as to what behaviors you're requesting of him.

Use positive reinforcement when training your pup for the behaviors you want. Praise and treats will be much more motivating for him than verbal or physical reprimands.

Structure your puppy's daily routines. Dogs thrive on the status quo.

CHAPTER SIX

House-Training Your GSD

You'd think a simple request like "Please don't poop in my kitchen" wouldn't be too difficult to follow. And yet, simple as it is, your German Shepherd Dog may have a difficult time with it. Physical elimination is as natural to a puppy as sniffing and yawning—they're all just everyday bodily functions. So, when you start his potty

As soon as you bring home your puppy, take him to his designated potty area in the backyard.

training, your puppy will be wondering what your hang-up is with all the urination and defecation.

When it comes down to it, house training is a case of humans trying to make a canine understand our standard rules of order. We want our homes to remain clean and odor-free, and puppies don't always seem to share this immediate desire. The fact, however, is that dogs are actually very clean animals. They naturally refrain from eliminating where they eat or sleep; however, their areas of choice may not be the same as yours. Therefore, it's going to take consistency, fast action, and a whole lot of patience on your part to make the house-training sink in.

CRATE TRAINING

From reading our previous chapters, you know to purchase a good-sized wire crate for your puppy that will be used for much more than just the occasional naptime getaway, a cookie-munching haven, or for safety on long trips in the car. The crate will also be your answer to a clean kitchen (and living room and dining room, and so forth).

Some dog owners have made up their minds about crates and will want to skip over this section because they feel bad putting dogs in crates, as though they are locking them up behind bars. However, there is nothing inhumane or jail-like about using a crate properly. A crate is like a safe den for your GSD, and a puppy would much rather sleep contentedly in his clean crate than deal with his owner's anger for piddling on the dining room carpet.

The whole notion of crate-training comes from our knowledge that canines are den-dwelling creatures. Their ancestors dug holes in the ground, hollowed out sides of large trees, or abandoned caves to sleep in and sometimes deliver and care for their young. Wolves and foxes don't defecate in their dens—canines are naturally clean creatures, grooming themselves and keeping their sleeping and eating places immaculately clean. You don't have to train your German Shepherd puppy not to pee in his crate; he naturally does not want to soil his bed. You must simply know how to use the crate correctly to get the results you want.

Introduce your puppy to his crate on his first day home. Allow him to inspect the crate with the door open. Don't be surprised if he settles down in there with a toy or a bone. If your puppy ignores the crate, then entice him toward it with a tasty treat. Toss the cookie into the crate and let him retrieve it. Praise him for doing so. When he enters the crate, say something like "Good crate" or "Good kennel." Make sure that your puppy's first associations with the crate are positive. You can feed your puppy a special meal in his open crate, or you can incorporate the crate into a game of "Find Your Toy" (see page 60).

During the course of the day, place the puppy in his crate for short naps. He will get used to the crate little by little. If you can keep an eye on him while he naps, then you don't even need to close the crate door. But if you won't be nearby, close the crate door. As soon as your puppy awakens from his nap, scoop him up and take him outside. The first thing a puppy does after waking up is urinate. Young puppies under twelve weeks of age will need to go every hour. That could mean a dozen potty trips to keep your house pee-free. This part of dog ownership truly requires a commitment, as well as some good disinfectant and a strong back.

When it's time for bed, you should announce "Good crate" and lure your dog in. If you're ready for bed before he is, simply pick up your pup, kiss him good

Water Works

Remove your puppy's water bowl in the early evening, at least a couple of hours prior to bedtime. This will make it easier for your puppy to control his bladder through the night. If it's a hot night or the puppy shows signs of thirst, give him an ice cube to lick. Your German Shepherd will enjoy playing ice hockey with his nose on your floor, and he'll look forward to your visits to the freezer in the future. Don't overdo the ice, though, or your puppy will have an accident in his crate overnight.

A PIECE OF HISTORY

Legendary dog trainer Carl Spitz emigrated from Germany to California to become the Hollywood movie dog-training master. A student of Col. Konrad Most, Spitz trained Rin Tin Tin at his Hollywood Dog Training School, which he opened in 1927. In addition to that famous German Shepherd Dog, Spitz also trained the Cairn Terrier named Terry who portrayed "Toto" for the MGM film *The Wizard of Oz* in 1939 and the St. Bernard named Buck in *Call of the Wild* starring Clark Gable. Spitz is also credited for setting up the World War II War Dog Program and was involved in classified K9 units and commando programs.

night, and place him in his crate. If you want, give your pup a small cookie as you close the door of the crate. Because your puppy has been enjoying your company for hours now, he inevitably will express his dislike for these sleeping arrangements. He will whine, squeal, bark, and otherwise carry on until you come running back to the crate, comfort him, let him out, and carry him to your bed. Don't let this happen, or you will just be reinforcing the negative behavior.

If you're a softie, then visit him at his crate and comfort him with some encouraging words. If you're a super-softie, you can carry his crate into your bedroom and put him next to your bed. Your German Shepherd may take comfort in knowing that you are nearby. A puppy should be able to get through the whole night without needing to relieve himself, provided you stopped giving him water a full hour or two prior to bedtime. If the puppy does need a midnight potty run, you will be there to know it. Whatever you do, don't take him out of his crate and carry him into bed with you. The clean kennel rule does not apply to your queen-size bed and clean sheets. He'll have no problem peeing on your silk pillow and then sleeping by your feet!

Three Keys to House Training

It's nice to have an obedient German Shepherd Dog that will sit on command or even down-stay off-leash for sixty seconds, but it's not critical to your daily life. House-training, on the other hand, is critical, and it's at the top of the list of all behavior-controls that an owner must accomplish. The most important aspects of successful house-training are:

1. CONSISTENCY: Your puppy is relying on you to establish a routine and stick to it. House-training is only important to you, not the puppy. If you want your puppy to succeed (and you definitely do!), then make a real effort to tackle this first training hurdle. Decide on a plan of action for how you want your dog to behave, then stick to it in your training.

2. REPETITION: German Shepherds are creatures of habit and need to understand what's expected of them. An owner can ingrain into his dog what is expected by repeating the same commands, doing the same routine day after day until the puppy responds without failure.

3. WORD ASSOCIATION: Decide on the words you will use for house-training methods, and be consistent. "Go crate," "Outside," and "Go potty" are three of the most common phrases owners use to communicate with their dogs when it's time to go.

Use the same door to go outside to the potty area, and your GSD will head for the door when he has to go.

Paper Training

Most dog trainers encourage owners to refrain from using puppy pee pads or paper for indoor eliminating when you intend on eventually teaching your dog to go potty outside. It'll only confuse him. Granted, some living situations require indoor potty training. But German Shepherd Dogs are big and active and might not be conducive to apartment dwelling anyway.

If you're determined to house-train your dogs indoors, set the pad or papers in a designated area where you want your puppy to go. Then place him on this spot when he looks like he needs to eliminate and praise him when he's done. If you're having trouble training your pup to return to the correct spot, try wiping some of his urine on the paper or pee pad to attract him to the scent.

THE CALL OF NATURE

Choose a location in your backyard where you want your puppy to do his business. Then grab his leash and collar, and lead him to this spot outside and encourage him to go. Choose a command like "Potty" or "Let's go pee," and use it every time you take the puppy out. Structure and consistency are extremely important in house-training a puppy. The puppy wants to learn a routine so he knows what's expected of him. If possible, always use the same door to take the puppy outside. If time permits, attach the collar and leash; if it's an emergency, whisk the puppy up and get him outside. Your puppy will soon know which door he uses to go outside, and he will head for the door when he knows it's time. Even when they start to catch on, puppies don't give you much advanced notice. It may take only a few seconds from the first sign that your pup has to go to the arrival of the actual stream that follows. As your pup gets older, the window of opportunity

Constructive Crating

Remember that your puppy must always associate his crate with good times. As tempting and convenient as it may be, do not scold the puppy for a misdeed and then "send him to his room" (aka, a time out). If you must place your puppy in his crate to keep him from getting underfoot or simply to keep him out of the way for a half hour, then do it in a positive manner. Place the puppy in his crate calmly and tell him "Now be a good boy." The crate is a handy holding zone for your puppy while you're cleaning up a mess (or putting the kitchen garbage back in the can). Never be angry when you place your puppy in his crate. If he begins to associate the crate with punishment or reprimands, he won't regard it as his safe haven.

Keep potty and play time outdoors separate. Make sure your GSD understands when it's time to do his business and when he gets to play and explore.

widens, and you'll actually get the pup outside in time instead of ending up with a puddle or a warm, wet shirt.

If you're lucky enough to catch your puppy piddling indoors, take that opportunity to correct him so he understands that urination in the house is not permitted. Make sure your GSD knows that peeing displeases you, but don't overdo it. Keep in mind that you actually have to catch the puppy in the act in order for a correction to have any effect. Some experts say you only have four seconds from the time of the unwanted behavior to correcting it. If you correct the puppy three minutes after he's relieved himself, he won't understand why you're upset.

Do not ever use physical force to correct your puppy. Never hit your German Shepherd Dog for relieving himself indoors. All you ever accomplish by hitting a dog is the loss of his trust. And that's the worst thing an owner/trainer can do.

GATES

Don't allow your GSD puppy to have the run of the house at ten weeks old. If it's your intention to allow your dog "full access" to your home, then let him earn it room by room, as he proves to be consistent in his house-training and good behavior. Never allow a puppy into rooms where he can chew up your furniture; better to confine him to a general family area where he can be supervised.

Purchase a couple of sturdy baby (or puppy) gates to section-off rooms or areas of your home to confine the puppy. Because they will be temporary fixtures in your home, you don't have to purchase the most expensive gates on the market. Just look for ones that are sturdy and strong enough to do the job.

Gates are not substitutes for crates, but they are very helpful for puppy-proofing the home. If your home layout doesn't lend itself to baby gates in doorways, you can also look into exercise pens, which usually measure about 4 to 6 feet square. These pens create a safe area for your puppy to play.

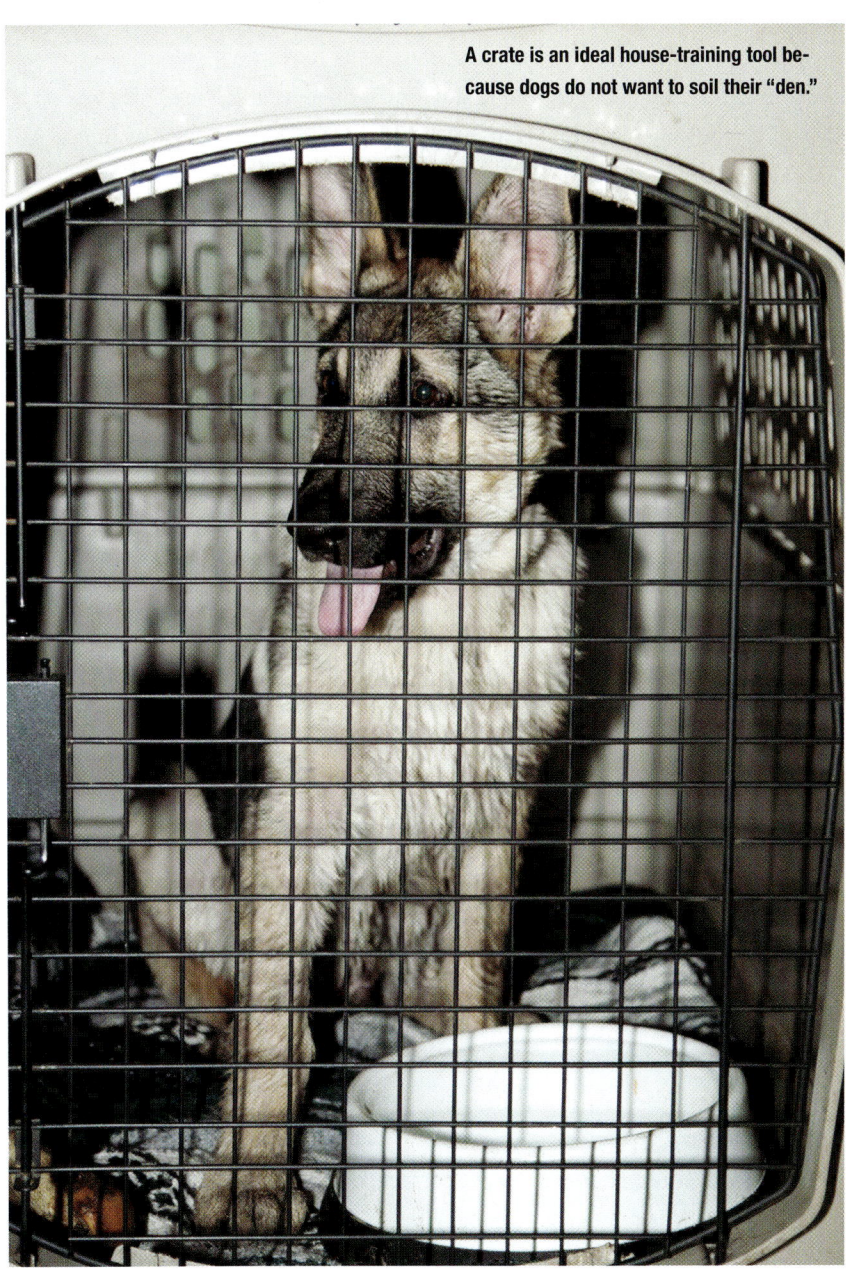

A crate is an ideal house-training tool because dogs do not want to soil their "den."

Home Cleaning Solutions

Your pup will inevitably have a few (or many!) accidents while house-training. Luckily, you can use many household items to help keep your home clean during this training stage.

■ If you don't have any professional cleaners on hand, create your own using ¼ cup of white vinegar to 1 quart of water.

■ Salt will absorb fresh urine and remove some of the scent.

■ In a pinch, rubbing the area with a dryer sheet can remove some of the odor.

■ White toothpaste can sometimes remove some tough stains from carpet. But beware—it can also ruin the carpet's coloring! It's best never to use toothpaste on dark-colored carpets.

House-Training Your GSD **69**

Personal Space

Every dog needs to have his own designated place to rest. Having a place to escape from potentially stressful situations, where the dog is able to relax undisturbed, provides psychological comfort. The personal space can be a corner of the living rooms, a crate, or even just a pad or blanket that you move between room and bring on your travels. When your puppy gets tired and starts to fall asleep, put him on his bed. In a few days, he will probably start going there on his own when he feels sleepy.

Most importantly, when your GSD is in his personal place, he should feel safe from harassment. Although a dog should passively allow himself to be handled by familiar people when on his bed, never touch any sleeping dog without announcing yourself verbally and making sure he recognizes you. He may have just been dreaming of defending himself from another dog and snap at an unexpected touch.

Many crate-haters are gate-lovers, which makes sense. For some destructive GSD toddlers and adolescents, puppy-proofing is never enough. A bored German Shepherd can find something to chew up even in the most stripped-down environment. Owners regularly exchange "war-zone" stories about puppies that have eaten through drywall, scratched their way through wooden doors, or removed and devoured decorative molding, wainscoting panels, and worse. To a degree, gates will contain a destructive puppy, but firm, fair obedience training is what you really need. Some creative puppies also develop remarkable Houdini skills and learn to escape any enclosure, including a wire crate.

KNOW YOUR PUPPY'S LIMITATIONS

While house-training, always keep in mind that you are essentially dealing with a baby. The crate can be a great teaching tool, but be sure to limit the amount of time you keep your puppy in it. Except for during the night when the puppy sleeps for longer stretches, use this rule of thumb to calculate how long to keep your GSD in his crate: match the number of hours to your puppy's age—so three hours for a three-month-old, four hours for a four-month-old, etc. For puppies under twelve weeks old, two hours in the crate is the limit. And for dogs six months or older, six hours is the maximum. The same goes for penning your pup behind a gate. He may have more room to roam around in, but that just means more places to have an accident. If no one in your household can come home to let your GSD out during the day while you're at work or school, ask a neighbor or friend to stop by to let the dog out to go to the bathroom and get some exercise.

Remember: house-training is best taught by repeating the same actions and commands and by watching your puppy closely. The more you show your pup where to go potty, the more he will remember to go in the right place. Most of all, your GSD wants to make you happy; so be patient and let him know that you still love him, even when he makes mistakes.

During house-training, use the same word or phrase every time you take your German Shepherd outside.

At a Glance ...

House training will be the biggest—and most important—hurdle that you will have to cross as a new GSD puppy owner. Show your pup immediately where you want him to go potty.

Take your pup to his designated potty area the moment you bring him home from the breeder. Praise and reward him for going in the correct area, then repeat...repeat...repeat!

You will only have a few moments to get your puppy outside after you see signs that he needs to go. If you don't act fast enough and he has an accident indoors, focus on doing a better job next time and do not punish your dog.

A crate is a great house-training tool because dogs love to have a quiet place of their own, and they naturally don't want to eliminate near where they sleep.

If you decide not to use a crate, then invest in a sturdy pet gate to contain your pup to a single, safe area while you are away from home.

CHAPTER SEVEN
Home Care for the GSD

A happy, healthy German Shepherd Dog requires constant care and attention. Your dog's main requirements in life will be proper diet, exercise, and grooming. As he grows, he'll need exercise and plenty of it. And all that activity requires enough fuel to keep him going. The right food balanced with vitamins, minerals, and nutrients will help keep your German Shepherd in the best condition possible, inside and out.

Homemade Food

Entirely home-made diets are gaining popularity. If you choose to feed your German Shepherd Dog raw bones and meat with biologically appropriate foods such as raw fruits and vegetables, don't experiment on your own. It's far too easy for such diets to have too much or too little of some nutrient, resulting in poor health and growth abnormalities. Use recipes devised by dietary experts such as veterinary nutritionists (available in books and on the Internet) and GSD breeders who have raised at least two generations of dogs on the diet. Some deficiencies are subtle and manifest only in the offspring, so inter-generational trials are necessary to prove a food is sufficient.

WHAT TO FEED

Start by feeding your puppy the same diet he received from his breeder or previous owner. If you want to change your dog's diet, do so in small stages by replacing one-fourth of the original food with the new food each day. Rapid changes, or getting a large amount of an unfamiliar food, especially a rich or spicy one, can cause vomiting or diarrhea.

The German Shepherd's dietary needs call for a complete and balanced mix of proteins, carbohydrates, fats, vitamins, and minerals. Not to mention, plenty of water to wash it all down. When scouring the store shelves, look for foods that are labeled as "complete and balanced" by the Association of American Feed Control Officials (AAFCO), which has standardized the requirements for appropriate canine food formulas. Manufacturers earn this label either by conducting strictly controlled feeding trials or by matching their products to a well-detailed nutrient profile.

Most concerned owners of GSDs choose to feed quality dry kibble preserved with natural antioxidants as the basic diet and adding other ingredients suitable for the dog's life stage and activity level. Dry kibble is by far the cheapest, and the crunchy texture helps remove the plaque and tartar from dogs' teeth. It is also more calorie- and nutrient-dense. There are a few exceptions, but most soft-moist dog foods contain artificial preservatives and high levels of sugar. Some canned foods are excellent, but they are about 70 percent water by weight, and feeding quality canned diets can become very expensive.

If you choose to feed kibble, dogs sometimes prefer for it to be soaked with warm water until it is soft but not mushy. Add water just to the top of the kibble in your dog's bowl, and let it sit until the water is absorbed: the time required varies according to the density of the kibble.

Beware of Bloat

GSDs and other large, deep-chested breeds, are susceptible to bloat, a deadly condition in which the entrance and/or exit of the stomach becomes blocked. It has been suggested that the risk of bloat is decreased if the dog eats dry kibble and then drinks adequate water for its digestion. Self-feeding or free-feeding (leaving out dry food all the time) is not recommended for any dog. Dogs' systems are adapted to large, infrequent meals. Adult dogs can survive if fed just one large meal a day, but beware that this raises the risk of bloat. It's better to feed two smaller meals daily. Providing specified meal times gives your dog something to look forward to at least twice a day, and knowing when the dog will be hungriest permits the owner to pick the most receptive times for positive-reward training, i.e., before meals or half way through the day.

Puppy Diets

German Shepherd puppies go through a tremendous growth period from two to nine months of age. During this time, they need excellent nutrition with ample protein. A meat-based adult kibble (the first ingredient on the food label is the name of the meat—beef, chicken, lamb—not "meal" or "by-products") or puppy kibble for large-breed dogs are excellent choices for a base diet. Most puppies are fine eating only kibble. However, if you can supplement your pup's diet with cottage cheese (which is high in calcium, so don't overdo it), raw eggs, and raw or cooked vegetables and fruits like chopped broccoli, green beans, apples, or plums. *Note:* Never feed grapes, raisins, or chocolate; they contain substances that are toxic to dogs!

Feed three meals a day of whatever amount the breeder recommends for up to sixteen weeks of age, then reduce to two meals a day after that. Watch your puppy's weight, and add to the amount fed if his ribs become too visible. Feeding

Did You Know?

The German Shepherd Dog Club of America (www.gsdca.org) holds an annual National Specialty Show to showcase the various abilities of the highly renowned German Shepherd—from conformation to rally to herding. The event is held in a different location each year to attract as many German Shepherd Dog owners and lovers as possible.

Feeding Performance Dogs

Like human athletes, high-performance dogs need to eat a balanced high-energy diet. They are subject to greater wear and tear on their muscles and joints than the average dog, and the emotional and physical stress of competition can quickly deplete their reserves. In general, performance diets are higher in complete proteins and provide more energy per serving than average diets. If you have a performance dog, consult with your veterinarian, as well as books about canine athletes, nutritional literature, and people experienced with performance GSDs, before you decide the types and amounts of food your dog needs.

excess food so that your puppy becomes fat is absolutely the worst thing you can do to your fast-growing GSD puppy. It puts undue pressure on still-soft joints and immature tendons and ligaments. If you can't easily feel his ribs and hip bones or you can see rolls along his side when he trots, a doggy diet is in order. Reduce the overall amount your dog eats, but don't eliminate any single ingredient. Your dog will not thrive on a slow-carb regimen or any other fad diets.

If your GSD puppy starts to "knuckle over," meaning his pasterns ("wrists") are flexing so far forward that they no longer form a straight line with his front legs, this indicates he is growing so rapidly that his tendon and ligament strength cannot keep up with the lengthening of the forelegs' long bones. If you see this happening, consult your veterinarian or an experienced breeder (even one with another large breed) for advice.

Adult Diets

Adult GSD diets are usually based on a quality kibble, and they can benefit from the same supplements as mentioned above for puppies. You just increase the amount of kibble and decrease the relative proportion of protein. Adults need less protein than growing puppies, but more bulk food.

If your German Shepherd becomes too heavy, cut back on the calorie-dense kibble and replace it with cooked or raw green beans. If you can't easily feel your dog's ribs and he appears to have no "waist" when you look down at his back, you'll know it's time to cut back. Most dogs will accept the low-carbohydrate green beans when mixed in the meal; they add desirable fiber, which is low in most commercial foods. This makes the dog feel full and not get hungry again too soon.

You should be able to see (or feel) some weight loss by the end of the second week on the partial green bean diet. If not, cut the kibble back another half-cup to see if it results in a slow weight decrease, and continue that mix until you've achieved your dog's ideal weight. Whenever your GSD needs to lose weight (or to help keep him from gaining too much weight), try offering whole raw carrots or apples as "toys" instead of feeding high-calorie treats. Just be sure to feed them outside because they make a mess when chewed.

Older GSDs need fewer calories as they become less active. Their weight needs to be closely monitored, as excess weight is very damaging to an older dog's orthopedic health. Senior German Shepherds also need less protein than middle-aged GSDs, but it must be of a high quality because the dogs' aged digestive systems are less effective at extracting nutrients.

EXERCISE

All dogs need exercise in order to live a healthy life. Small dogs get enough exercise just running and jumping throughout the house, but adequately exercising a large dog like the GSD requires planning and owner participation. As puppies, they need regular exercise to develop into strong, healthy adults. As adults, they need regular exercise in order to stay physically and mentally fit. Although fit adult German Shepherds relish long hikes and jogs with you, don't fret if you are not highly athletic. If you are not physically able or do not have the time to participate personally in your dog's exercise activities, make arrangements for someone else to do so, such as a professional dog walker or a capable friend.

Until at least a year of age, the ends of the shepherd's leg bones are not completely calcified, and are prone to injury. Puppies need controlled, gradually increased, gentle exercise as they mature because their fast-growing bones can be damaged by severe exercise or stresses such as jumping up and down higher than their height at the shoulder. Use common sense when exercising your GSD puppy; don't let him engage in very strenuous running, twisting, and jumping.

All that a younger puppy really needs are a few regular short play sessions a day involving some ball chasing and supervised yard time. Mature GSDs need a minimum of 30 minutes of moderate physical activity daily. Such exercises can range from practicing obedience or agility, accompanying their owners on brisk walks or jogs, chasing a ball in the backyard or on a long leash in a park, playing with supervised children, or anything that gets the dog actively moving around without endangering his physical well-being. If your adult German Shepherd Dog is a bit pudgy, increase his exercise slowly while the dog's condition improves to avoid

Free Food

Leave your dog's food bowl full round the clock, and he could turn into a picky eater—a bite here, a nibble there. Dogs that are free-feeders are also more likely to become possessive of their food bowls. If you come near your dog's bowl, he could begin growling at you, which is a dog's way of saying "Back off!" Dogs should never growl at their owners, as it could lead to other more serious behavioral problems of aggression. Not to mention the risk of obesity with a dog too food-driven to self-regulate his own rations. Instead, dole our smaller portions of your dog's food a couple of times throughout the day. It will make your German Shepherd grateful to you for providing food and enable you to keep better track of exactly how much he's consuming.

Dog Grooming Shopping List

Here are the items you need to groom your German Shepherd Dog:

BATHING
- A handheld spray attachment for your tub or sink
- A rubber mat for the dog to stand on
- A tearless dog shampoo and conditioner (don't use human products)
- Towels (a chamois is best)
- A pet hair dryer (you can use your own, but set it on cool)
- Spritz-on dry shampoos (handy in case you need a quick clean-up to get rid of dirt or odor)

BRUSHING COAT
- Soft pin brush or slicker brush
- Metal comb

TRIMMING NAILS
- Dog nail cutters (scissor- or guillotine-type)
- Nail file (to file down jagged edges)
- Styptic powder (in case you cut the quick)

BRUSHING TEETH
- Dog toothbrush or child's toothbrush
- Dog toothpaste (don't use human toothpaste)

CLEANING EARS
- Cotton balls or wipes
- Liquid ear-cleaning solution

WIPING EYES
- Doggie eye wipes or hydrogen peroxide
- Cotton balls

Your German Shepherd loves outdoor adventures, but when you get home, go through your regular grooming routine—brushing and checking his ears and nails.

stressing the joints. Don't allow your dog to jump up or down higher than his height at the shoulder until he is slender once again. If you can't easily feel the dog's ribs, it's a good indication that he needs to lose some weight.

GROOMING

German Shepherd Dogs are double-coated canines, with an outer water-resistant coat and a short, felt-like undercoat that is very dense in cold seasons. Luckily, this type of coat can be maintained with only moderate effort on your part. Like all animals with fur, GSDs shed a little year-round as hairs are replaced. Twice yearly, in the spring and less so in the fall, the dog's undercoat will shed and grooming needs to be more frequent during those seasons.

Beyond coat care, overall general care and maintenance of your German Shepherd's body—inside and out—also consists of bathing, dental care, and nail care. Read on for further information.

Brushing

Introduce your German Shepherd to grooming at a young age. Using a soft-bristle brush, comb in the direction the hair grows or else it will be an unpleasant experience for your dog. If you keep the experience positive when he's a pup, then he will calmly accept his grooming sessions as an adult. Adult GSDs need to be thoroughly brushed a minimum of once a week: head to tail, down to the skin. More frequent brushing is always better. Before each grooming session, give your GSD a vigorous finger massage, which will benefit his coat and skin.

The most useful overall grooming tool for German Shepherds is a fine-wire slicker brush that can gather loose hairs from both the under and outer coat. In spring, a narrow-toothed "rake" can be used to get the majority of the undercoat out, followed by the wire slicker. A stiff bristle brush should be used on your shepherd's face and legs in the direction the hair grows, and over his whole body to finish grooming. This grooming regimen stimulates the oil glands, loosens the hair ready to come out, and results in a gleaming coat.

Bathing

If you brush your GSD regularly, he won't need many baths because a healthy coat has little odor. No dog should be bathed more than once every week or two. Too-frequent baths will predispose the dog to skin problems. Introduce your pup to bathing in the bathtub or sink using lukewarm water. Be patient yet firm while giving your dog his first few baths, and always avoid washing his face. If you start early, your dog will be used to the process by the time he gets big enough to really put up a fight while bathing.

Get your puppy used to grooming with short sessions of brushing his coat every week from the time you bring him home.

When it does come time to bathe your German Shepherd, brush through his coat completely to remove as much loose hair as possible. Then completely wet the coat, massaging dog shampoo through all parts of the coat, and rinsing down to the skin. Wetting and rinsing an adult GSD's coat takes some effort because of the undercoat. Make certain that all of the shampoo is completely removed from your dog's coat because any left in will create skin problems. Your dog will shake as soon as you release him from the bath, throwing water everywhere. Keep a towel nearby, ready to toss over your dog's back. Rub your dog briskly with several large towels, which will absorb most of the water from his coat. A chamois (a special kind of towel people use most often to dry cars) works well because it absorbs water like a sponge. Then his fur can be air dried or dried with a canine or human hair dryer set to low.

Ear Cleaning

Keeping your puppy's ears clean and healthy should be a part of your grooming routine. Look down into both ears and massage them at the base while praising your pup. Give him a treat if he holds still for this handling. Use a soft cloth wrapped around your finger to wipe gently around in the puppy's ears, even if there is nothing to clean out. This early conditioning will teach your puppy to be cooperative when he needs his ears cleaned.

The large ears of the GSD are like funnels, collecting dust and dirt. Even folded down ears may get dirt in them if your dog rolls around on the ground.

Check your GSD puppy's ears at least once a week, looking inside (use a flashlight if necessary) and smelling them. A minor amount of dirt accumulation in the outer folds is of no concern, but a build-up of dark, moist wax needs to be tended to. Buy an ear-cleaning solution at the pet-supply store, and fill your dog's ear canal with the cleaning solution. Then massage the base of the ears. Your dog will probably shake his head a few times, which is good because it forces the deep dirt out of the lower ear canal.

After your German Shepherd has shaken his head a few times, sit in a chair and have him sit in front of you. Keep your dog under control by putting him on a leash. Remember to reward his cooperation with praise and an occasional treat. This is the perfect time to clean your dog's ears. Wrap a soft cloth around your finger and wipe the inside of the ear, starting at the outermost section and working down so you do not push dirt farther down the canal. Go only as deep as you can easily see: never probe into the lower canal with any object. Cotton swabs can be used to remove dirt from the small folds inside the upper portion of the ear, but never push them into the lower canal.

If your dog has been scratching his ears, rubbing them on the floor or shaking his head a lot, check his ears. If his ears smell like something sour or musty, or if you see yellowish pus or an inflamed canal, take your dog to the veterinarian and have him checked for ear mites or an infection.

German Shepherds have big ears, which means they accumulate a lot of dirt. Check your dog's ears regularly and clean them whenever you see any dirt.

Conditioning Your GSD

If you plan to take your German Shepherd Dog jogging with you or to work him in any dog sports, you first need to ensure he is in excellent physical condition, and don't start until he is at least one year of age. Start slowly and progress to more strenuous levels of physical exertion in small steps. Make activities like fetching a ball more strenuous by using a simple device to throw it longer distances. If you decide to road work your dog (have him trot, not run, for long distances alongside while you jog or ride a bicycle) start by taking him only for a half-mile outing. Constantly observe your dog while he is exercising, and stop at the first sign of distress. Because GSDs are so willing to cooperate, they will over-exert themselves to please you, resulting in muscle and orthopedic problems.

Nail Clipping

Unless your German Shepherd regularly runs on hard ground, he will need nail clipping. If you hear your dog's nails clicking on the wood floors when he walks, they are too long. Excessively long nails are uncomfortable and can get caught on things and break.

Dog nails have a "quick," a soft center that is rich in blood vessels and nerves. Because GSDs usually have dark nails, the quick is not visible like it is in dogs with light-colored nails. When viewing the nail from the side, the quick usually ends where the nail becomes more slender and starts to hook over. As you near the quick, the oval center of the nail becomes soft; that is where you stop clipping. If you accidentally cut the quick, it will bleed. Have some blood-stop powder (styptic powder or stick) on hand. You can also try corn starch or flour to get the blood to clot.

Start acclimating your pup to having his feet handled and nails clipped as soon as he's settled into his new home. Play with his feet for short sessions. The point of these exercises is to make foot handling and nail clipping just a normal part of your puppy's life, a time when by just holding still can earn rewards.

If the ends of the nails are ragged or sharp after clipping, you can smooth them with a nail file. Draw the file down over the tip of the nail from top to bottom, rounding it out. There are nail files specifically made coarser for dogs' nails. Wood files can also be used on larger GSD's nails.

Nails can also be ground down rather than clipped. Before trying to grind your dog's nails, get him used to the sight, sound, and vibration of the rotary tool in small stages, rewarding him for calm behavior around it. Bring the tool around your dog in stages, first touching him with it turned off, then turning it on nearby while giving him a treat, and eventually working up to touching his nails with it turned on, until he's ready to accept the actual grooming. This process may take a while and will involve lots of patience and treats. Once he allows you to touch him with the tip on the tool, barely touch it to his nail, to see how fast the nail will grind. Then re-touch the grinder to the tip until you have reduced the nail to just before the quick. Be sure not to grind into the quick, or your dog will associate pain with the tool and the desensitization process will be more difficult.

Tooth Care

Too often, German Shepherd Dog owners fail to consider the condition of their dogs' teeth or provide any dental care. Ask your veterinarian to take a look at your dog's teeth at every visit, because he may notice potential problems that can lead to serious illness. Some GSDs' teeth develop tartar because they are kept on commercial dog food, which is often soft and does not require much chewing. A raw bone is the most natural tooth brush for a German Shepherd. These bones can be from any large mammal, but readily available beef bones are most commonly used. Give your dog two decently sized bones a week to provide enough gnawing to scrape off the film that becomes tartar. Never give your dog cooked bones of any kind because they can splinter apart rather than break off in small chunks and flakes like raw bones. Splinters of bone can get stuck in the dog's

Introduce your GSD to grooming at an early age. If you keep grooming sessions positive and fun, your dog will learn to love his weekly brush.

Ear Check

When dogs play outdoors, foreign objects sometimes get stuck in their ears, such as seeds, burrs, and foxtails—anything that tends to stick to fur. Check your German Shepherd's ears for these things when he comes in from playing outdoors. If left in the ear, they will cause your dog pain and possibly damage his hearing. If you find something in his ear and cannot safely remove it at home, take your dog to the veterinarian ASAP.

throat or potentially penetrate the dog's gut lining and cause infections. Hard, crunchy dog biscuits are another great tool in the arsenal against oral disease. The crunchy texture scrapes the tooth, helping to prevent tartar formation, and they can be given as a reward. However, if your GSD gains weight easily, keep in mind that bones and biscuits add calories.

To maintain your dog's dental health, you must brush your dog's teeth three or four times a week in addition to providing treats and bones. Most dogs learn to accept toothbrushing if you slowly acclimate them to the brush and reward them often with praise and treats for a job well done. There are several different styles of dog toothbrushes, but if you can't find one, a soft-bristle child's brush can also be used. However, do *not* give your dog your mint-flavored human toothpaste; it can make him sick. Look for meat-flavored dog toothpastes. While brushing, be sure to massage your dog's gums, while scrubbing away any food particles on his teeth. Be sure not to press so hard that your dog's gums bleed. The idea is to help your dog—not hurt him.

GROOMING HEALTH CHECK

Consider your dog's grooming sessions as an opportunity to take mental evaluation of his overall health and well being. Note any changes in his appetite or water intake. And search for any out-of-the-ordinary lumps or abrasions while brushing his coat. That way, if you do discover any abnormalities, you can visit the veterinarian for a checkup to avoid the development of any serious ailments. Your constant care and attention to your German Shepherd Dog's dietary and grooming needs will ensure you have a happy, healthy, beautiful dog by your side.

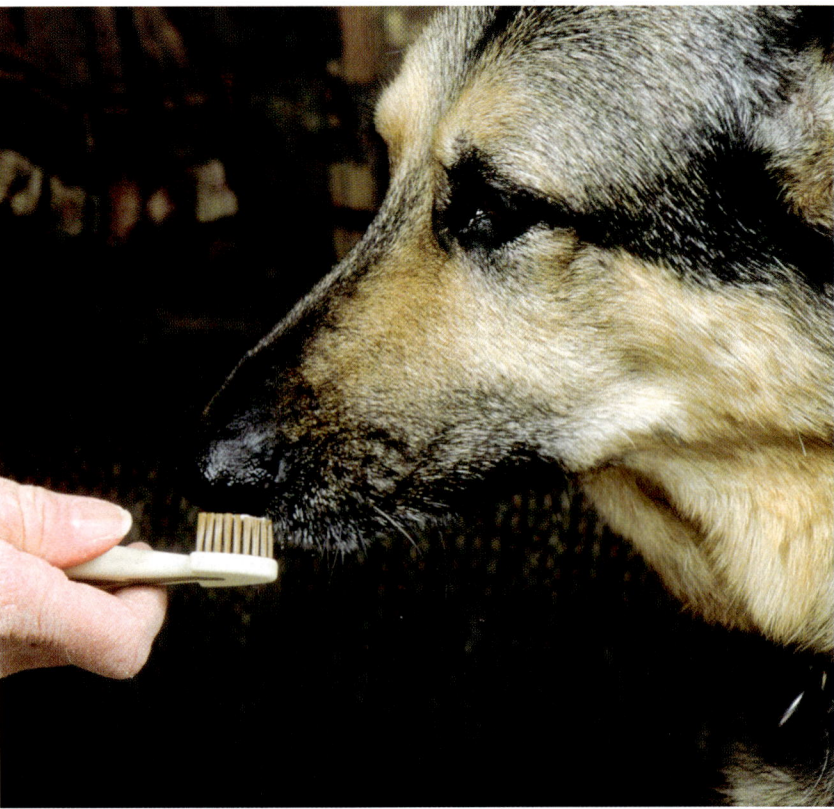

One of the most overlooked grooming tasks is toothbrushing. Dental health is vital for all dogs—brush your GSD's teeth every other day.

At a Glance ...

Consult your veterinarian and your puppy's breeder when deciding what food to feed him. If you decide to feed something other than what his breeder has been giving him, make the change gradually by adding a little of the new food each day until he is eating only the new diet.

Look for "complete and balanced" dog food formulas. They're federally regulated to contain all the necessary nutrients for your dog at any given stage of life.

The GSD requires relatively little grooming, beyond regular brushing and nail and teeth care.

During regular grooming sessions, check your German Shepherd for any lumps, bumps, or scratches.

CHAPTER EIGHT

GSD Command Central

What qualities of the German Shepherd Dog led you to select this breed? Did you see one trotting around a show ring on the televised AKC/Eukanuba National Championship? Was it the impressive sight of a seeing eye dog assisting his owner on a street corner? Maybe you were moved by search and rescue dogs that worked at Ground Zero in New York and the Pentagon in Washington, D.C. after September 11th. Perhaps

you simply met a well-mannered and beautiful German Shepherd at a friend's house while visiting.

Whatever qualities that have brought you to owning a GSD, you are now more than aware that this is no ordinary canine. This dog possesses unique qualities of intelligence, trainability, loyalty, versatility, and instinct that make him a dog among dogs. Owners are responsible for making sure that their GSDs become all they can be: whether that's an outstanding show dog, obedience contender, assistance dog, search and rescue dog, or simply a well-trained family pet.

Every German Shepherd should grow up to be able to take the Canine Good Citizen® test, as a well-behaved good canine citizen. All dog owners benefit from other owners taking responsibility for their dogs' manners and obedience training. Because our society isn't unanimously pro-dog, it's imperative that all dog lovers do their part to further the cause of dog ownership. Anti-dog legislation, often breed-specific, crops up in every state these days. It doesn't matter whether you own a pit bull-cross or a Chihuahua: these anti-dog agendas affect everyone. While you don't need to get political and hold a demonstration at your state capital, you do need to train your German Shepherd Dog so that he's reliable and always under your control. A dog that can sit, stay, heel, and come on call will be welcomed and admired wherever he goes.

Few dogs are as naturally bright and eager to learn as the German Shepherd, so you are blessed with a good student that is ready for his lessons.

A well-trained GSD is a sight to behold. It is your responsibility to raise your German Shepherd as a good canine citizen.

POSITIVE TRAINING

The first step in training is to find rewards (reinforcements) that are meaningful to your dog. High on the list for most dogs are food treats, and these are easy to find and use. Common high-value training treats are bits of cheese, chicken, cooked and partially dried liver, cooked hot dogs, and bits of really delicious dog cookies. However, a reward can be just about anything a dog likes that his human can supply. Some interactive behaviors are rewarding for dogs (such as chasing something, playing tug-of-war and other games, etc.), and the chance to engage in those behaviors can be used as a reward for complying with your command. Try out different treats and play or praise interactions, and make a list of what your dog prefers.

When introducing new commands or asking your dog to ignore some distraction in order to respond to a known command, use the top two or three rewards that your German Shepherd most desires. The key is for the trainer to become more attractive than the distraction, meaning the pay-off for obeying must be worth more to the dog than responding to the distraction. Slowly phase out food rewards until they are given only intermittently, being replaced most of

Your German Shepherd wants to please you, so make sure all training sessions are positive.

the time by rewards farther down the list. Praise and attention are usually reward enough for your GSD when the behavior has become a habit.

While your dog is in training, refrain from giving him any rewards except when he responds to a request. This increases the reward's motivational value; rewards given too often, including petting and praise, may lose appeal. When you reward with food, give very small pieces, about one quarter-inch across or no bigger than half the size of your smallest fingernail. If the pieces are too large, your dog will fill up quickly and lose motivation.

A PIECE OF HISTORY

German Shepherd Dogs are often portrayed in television and cinema. Rin Tin Tin, Strongheart, and Bullet from the *Roy Rogers Show* were only a few German Shepherd Dogs of Hollywood fame that helped propel the GSD to the second most popular breed in the United States.

Poisoned Cues

A "cue" is a word, body movement, or other clear signal that tells your dog what behavior you want him to perform. Cues become weak and useless—or poisoned—if the dog is allowed to ignore them. The most often poisoned cues are *come* and *stay*, because owners give the command when the dog is not ready or willing to obey, and they are not ready to enforce it. Convincing your dog that he must obey an already poisoned cue is much more difficult than ensuring the command does not become poisoned in the first place. When one cue (such as *come*) becomes damaged, it is often easier to substitute another cue rather than re-train the original.

SIT

This is the easiest command to teach, and it is the foundation for all that comes after. Get a food treat, let your dog smell it, and hold it just above your dog's nose. He should be in a standing position. Then, slowly move the treat back between your GSD's eyes. Most dogs readily sit in order to keep the treat in sight, and if yours starts to sit, say the marker word "yes" and then "sit." Reward as soon as your dog's rear is on the floor. If your German Shepherd backs up or moves away, try training in a corner. Avoid holding the food lure too high over your dog's head, or he will jump up to get it instead of sitting. It won't be long before you'll notice that your dog will go into the *sit* position when you sweep your hand in an upward movement, even without food. As soon your dog learns to follow your verbal signals, ask him to sit before he gets anything.

DOWN ON COMMAND

Begin this lesson with your dog sitting on a level surface. Show him the treat, then slowly move the lure downward from in front of his nose to the floor directly between his paws, or to just outside of one of his front paws. As your German Shepherd starts to let himself down to reach the treat, say "Yes, down!" and reward him when his chest touches the ground. If you move the treat too far in front of your dog's paws, your GSD will tend to get up and move toward the lure rather than going down.

If your dog does not respond to this type of luring, try sitting on the floor with one leg bent and lure your GSD to crawl under your leg As soon as your dog starts to lower his body, praise him by saying "Yes, down!" and reward him when he reaches a prone position. Only use the word "down" when you mean for your dog to lie down. Use another word such as "off" when you want your dog to stop jumping on people or to get off of furniture, or you will poison the *down* cue and confuse your dog.

COME ON COMMAND

The most important thing to remember when introducing this command to your dog is to never use the command word "come" until you have the dog's full attention and he is already moving toward you. When taught in this error-free way, the dog is never allowed to ignore the command, and coming when called becomes a strong habit. If your dog is too distracted to direct his attention to you, do not use the *come* cue to call him. Use another word such as "here" or just his name and some body language like clapping. If allowed to ignore the *come* command, the word will become a "poisoned cue" that the dog readily ignores.

Teaching the *come* command is straightforward. Say your dog's name so that he turns and makes eye contact with you, then show him a treat or toy. Hold the hand with the reward in it out toward the dog, and wave it in repeatedly toward your chest. If your dog hesitates, back up a little or bend over, even turn and trot a few paces away from the dog, to get him to come toward you. As your GSD starts to move closer, say "Yes, come" in a happy, uplifting tone. Give the reward and lots of praise when your dog reaches you.

STAY

Stay is an extremely useful command, but it is one of the most difficult to teach. The most important part of teaching the *stay* cue is to progress in tiny steps—extend the duration of the stay while adding distance from the dog, and then introduce distractions. Until your GSD can reliably stay for at least a minute, remain within arm's reach so you can correct your dog. End each duration of obeying the *stay* cue *before* your dog starts to move on his own. Going slowly in the beginning will result in a much more reliable *stay* command later on. Work on the *stay* command when your dog is calm and there are no distractions to draw his attention, such as children playing nearby or another animal. It is easier for some dogs to stay when they are tired, so a helpful trick is to take the dog out for a long walk or engage him in an energetic play session just prior to training.

Start with your dog either in a sit or down position, being sure to mark and reward if he obeys a command to get into position. Lean slightly toward the dog. As you look in his eyes, extend a hand, palm outward, fingers together, a foot or so from the dog's nose and say "stay" in a firm, deep voice. Do this all at once, rather than successively. Wait just one second, holding your palm toward the dog, then give a release word, such as "OK," and treat him. Your dog will learn that he must wait for your permission (the release word) before moving off that spot, if he wants a reward. A common mistake is to use praise as a releaser, which results in a dog that gets up when you or someone else uses praise words.

Using Visualizations

Before you start to train your GSD to follow any command, give some thought to exactly what it is you will be asking your dog to do. Envision the perfect response, such as a fast, straight sit, and then use that as the ideal you are working toward. If you are unsure of what you want the dog to do, this uncertainty may come across to the dog. Before you pick up the leash for a training session, stop and give some consideration to your goals and methods for that session, and review the lesson plan in your mind like a video on fast-forward. This technique is used by golfers, baseball players, dancers, and other athletes and is a proven aid to improve performance.

The Prime Directive

Rule number one in dog training is to make sure your dog can succeed. It is your job to set up each training situation in a way that leads your German Shepherd to the correct response. Motivating your dog is part of ensuring that he can succeed, so make training a fun game for your GSD and stop sessions before your dog is tired of the game.

Can Your Dog Pass the Canine Good Citizen® Test?

Once your German Shepherd Dog is ready for advanced training, you can start training him for the American Kennel Club Canine Good Citizen Program. This program is for dogs that are trained to behave at home, out in the neighborhood, and in the city. It's easy and fun to do. Once your dog learns basic obedience and good canine manners, a CGC evaluator gives your dog ten basic tests. If he passes, he's awarded a Canine Good Citizen certificate. Many trainers offer classes with the test as the final "graduation" class. To find an evaluator in your area, go to www.akc.org/events/cgc/cgc_bystate.cfm.

Many therapy dogs and guide dogs are required to pass the Canine Good Citizen test in order to help as working dogs in the community. There are ten specific tests that a dog must pass in order to pass the Canine Good Citizen test. A well-trained dog will:

1. Let a friendly stranger approach and talk to his owner.
2. Let a friendly stranger pet him.
3. Be comfortable being groomed and examined by a friendly stranger.
4. Walk on a leash and show that he is in control and not overly excited.
5. Move through a crowd politely and confidently.
6. Sit and stay on command.
7. Come when called.
8. Behave calmly around another dog.
9. Not bark at or react to a surprise distraction.
10. Show that he can be left with a trusted person away from his owner.

In order to help your dog pass the AKC CGC Program test, first enroll your dog in a series of basic training classes and CGC training classes. You can find classes and trainers near you by searching the AKC website. When you feel that your dog is ready to take the test, locate an AKC Approved CGC Evaluator to set up a test date, or sign up for a test that is held at a local AKC dog show or training class. For more information about the AKC Canine Good Citizen Program, visit the website at www.akc.org/events.cgc.

The first five or so stay exercises should be momentary, so the dog can't make a mistake. If necessary, you can gently place a non-signaling hand on the dog's shoulders to keep him steady during the first stays. Although practicing the stay position can and should be integrated into daily activities, a second here and another there, you can do up to three in succession. More than three repetitions will increase the odds that your German Shepherd will stop listening. Every ten or so times you practice the *stay* cue, add a second to the duration.

LOOSE-LEASH WALKING

The goal here is to teach your dog to walk on a slack leash without pulling. Introduce this behavior in short sessions, no more than for five minutes two or three times a day, to keep your dog motivated. At first, work indoors without distractions. When your dog willingly follows you around the house without pulling on the leash, you can start working in the yard, then on sidewalks, and finally in public places. Intersperse other commands between walking. Slowly increase the lesson length to about twenty minutes twice a day, which is about the time it takes for most dogs to start to get bored. If your GSD is already a puller, consider using a head halter to help overcome this problem.

Teaching loose-leash walking will make your GSD a much more pleasant companion. Use a leash about 6 feet long attached to the dog's regular flat collar or to a martingale collar that closes tight enough that the dog cannot back out, but loose enough not to choke him. The traditional position for walking a dog is for the person to be on the left side, but with this casual type of walking the dog can wander around a little, maybe pausing to sniff something now and again, as long as the leash stays slack. You can teach your dog to discriminate the command for casual walking, with cues such as "let's go" or "by me."

Training Log

Some trainers suggest keeping an on-going record of your progress. Having a log you can review keeps you on track, and you can refer back to see how your German Shepherd has improved even when it may not seem like he has. Also, it can be useful to note any trends, good or bad, and make appropriate adjustments to enhance or change your approach. Entries can be as simple as "Today, Fido sat three of the six times I asked him to, even though there was a loose dog distracting him."

Goals

You should have short-term, mid-term, and long-term goals in mind before you start working with your dog. A short-term goal (one that can be achieved in a few weeks) might be something like having your GSD sit and stay for one minute. A mid-term goal could be your dog keeping the leash loose while walking in a strange place. A long-term goal could be having your German Shepherd pass the AKC's Canine Good Citizen test, or participation in an organized dog sport, search and rescue, or passing the test to be a visiting therapy dog. Goals should be realistic at each level, because it is just as important for you to realize success as it is for your dog.

HEEL

"Heeling" is loose-leash walking with added limits to the dog's position. In heeling, the dog must stay within a foot or so of your left knee, neck level with your leg, and sit automatically when you stop. The complete attention required for heeling is tiring both for dog and handler.

The heel command is useful in situations such as asking your German Shepherd to heel if you will have to pass a strong distraction during a casual walk, such as when crossing paths with another person walking a dog. To shape the heel cue from loose-leash walking, have a treat ready in your right hand and

Once your German Shepherd masters heeling and the other basic training cues, try competing in obedience trials.

hold the leash in your left with just a little slack when the dog is sitting level with your left knee. Say the dog's name, then "heel," and step right off, keeping the dog's attention on either you or the treat. Talk happily, repeating affirmation like "Yes—good dog!" Walk a few steps at a brisk pace, then tell your dog to heel as you come to a stop, barely tightening the leash to stop the forward momentum. Mark with "Yes—good dog!" and reward with a treat or a chest rub.

Repeat this, gradually taking more steps in between stops, then adding right, left and about turns. If your dog gets more than a foot from your knee in any direction, repeat the heel command just as you turn away from your dog, then slap your left knee and encourage your GSD to catch up before the leash gets too tight. Never pull a dog back or try to pull him forward. This only triggers an opposite resistance in the dog and creates a battle where none is necessary. When you are walking, keep your right hand with the treats at your waist, and occasionally, lean over as you walk and give your dog the treat when he is in the correct position, thus rewarding the desired position.

FURTHER TRAINING

All of these behaviors are taught in a young-dog training class. To find an obedience class in your area, check with your veterinarian or local pet store or kennel club. Keep in the mind that the more knowledgeable you are about your dog's training, the more successful he will be. Enforce these cues by making them a part of your German Shepherd's daily routine.

If your GSD takes well to his training, there are endless ways to use it beyond merely in the home and around your neighborhood. First look into enrolling your pup in the AKC S.T.A.R. Puppy® Program, which will give your puppy a great foundation as a valued family companion. To find out more, visit www.akc.org/starpuppy. You can also search for a trainer who teaches the AKC's Canine Good Citizen Program (www.akc.org/events/cgc/index.cfm), which encourages responsible pet ownership and rewards dogs with good manners. From there, it's on to service or therapy work, or a variety of canine sports from obedience and conformation to agility and tracking. The AKC offers events in all of these sports, which we'll discuss in chapter 10.

Change Your Tone

Research has shown that dogs are very sensitive to the tone of voice used to interact with them. To a dog, a happy, high-pitched tone helps motivate them to move, to come toward you. Dams (mothers) use a high-pitched whine to call their puppies to them, and all dogs whine to call each other when they are in need of attention. Use this voice for action commands such as *come, sit,* and *heel.* In contrast, dogs perceive deep-toned voices, like the growl, to mean stop whatever behavior they are doing. So, use a deep, commanding tone for *down, no,* and *stay.*

At a Glance ...

Positive reinforcement has become the most popular training technique among dog trainers. Rather than punishing your German Shepherd for his negative behavior, create incentives and rewards for him to want to behave correctly.

When teaching your dog verbal cues for certain behaviors, remember to speak clearly and directly. And repeat, repeat, repeat!

The American Kennel Club's S.T.A.R. Puppy Program and Canine Good Citizen test are great tools for directing and gauging your GSD's level of training. With constant practice and patience, your dog will be a model citizen in no time.

CHAPTER NINE
Staying Healthy

As a responsible German Shepherd Dog owner, you must be committed to keeping your dog healthy. Luckily, the majority of GSDs are quite hardy and live to be ten or more years of age. Proactive healthcare also includes staying informed regarding common communicable diseases of dogs as well as external and internal parasites. Then you will be able to recognize symptoms and seek timely treatment before it becomes a major issue.

VETTING THE VET

The most important aspect of caring for your GSD's health is choosing a qualified veterinarian to work with. Once you have located a vet, continue to evaluate him or her with each visit. The best veterinarians are gentle but firm with their touch while handling animals and respectful toward both the owner and the dog. Part of respecting you as an owner is encouraging your questions and offering clear answers and explanations. A good vet won't be afraid to admit when he or she doesn't know something; there's no shame in looking something up or consulting with a colleague. If you come in with questions about your dog or with printouts from the Internet or other informational sources, a good veterinarian will admire your attempt to research possible diagnoses or treatments and will agree to look them over and discuss the implications with you.

Be sure to carefully follow any treatment plan that your veterinarian prescribes. If your German Shepherd is diagnosed with an unusual or difficult problem, one that may be disabling or life-threatening, consider getting a second opinion, if possible. Often veterinarians will recommend other vets who they respect for the second opinion.

GSD HEALTH CONCERNS

As one of the country's most popular breeds, German Shepherds and their health problems have been well-reported and documented over the last decades. The list of potential diseases affecting the breed is long, but that doesn't mean that the GSD is an unhealthy breed. All popular breeds have a long list of problems. Rarer breeds may have only a few medical problems listed, but that is due to the fact that they haven't been studied as extensively.

CORE Vaccines
Check with your vet, but all puppies should receive vaccines for the following diseases.

CONDITION	TREATMENT	PROGNOSIS	VACCINE NEEDED
ADENOVIRUS-2 (immunizes against Adenovirus-1, the agent of infectious canine hepatitis)	No curative therapy for infectious hepatitis; treatment geared toward minimizing neurologic effects, shock, hemorrhage, secondary infections	Self-limiting but cross-protects against infectious hepatitis, which is highly contagious and can be mild to rapidly fatal	Recommended
DISTEMPER	No specific treatment; supportive treatment (IV fluids, antibiotics)	High mortality rates	Highly recommended
PARVOVIRUS-2	No specific treatment; supportive treatment (IV fluids, antibiotics)	Highly contagious to young puppies; high mortality rates	Highly recommended
RABIES	No treatment	Fatal	Required

Take your dog to the vet for annual exams. It's best to catch an ailment in its early stages than to fight serious illness down the road.

Orthopedic problems, like hip and elbow dysplasia, are the most common medical problems seen in German Shepherds and other large, fast-growing breeds. These problems can be diagnosed with exams and x-rays. Nutritional management for your GSD (such as keeping puppies and adults fairly slim to prevent excessive joint stress, and supplementing with certain food additives and vitamins) can reduce the severity of these orthopedic problems.

The breed's parent club is a wealth of information for keeping your GSD healthy. Refer to the German Shepherd Dog Club of America's website (www.gsdca.com) for information on any hereditary health problems that breeders are concerned about.

PEST CONTROL

As a dog owner, there are certain truths that you just have to accept. You'll forever pick up your GSD's poop, see dog hair around the house even after vacuuming, and know that you'll be contending with fleas. Other less-common parasites are problematic, as well, but luckily they're all relatively easy to treat.

Fleas: As long as there have been dog owners to notice it, fleas have been a problem for dogs and other pets. Not only do they cause your dog to bite and scratch himself silly, but they can also cause disease. Your German Shepherd will

Did You Know?

Although most people refer to the dog simply as "German Shepherd," the breed's official name is "German Shepherd Dog." The breed was first registered under this name with the AKC in 1908.

Staying Healthy

undoubtedly get fleas at some point in his life, if not on more than one occasion. It's difficult to avoid because GSDs love to spend so much time outside—and fleas love to spend so much time on dogs! Luckily there are many ways to fight flea infestation. It may be difficult to prevent, but it is relatively simple to cure.

Because fleas travel on and off their hosts, you'll need to treat both your dog and your home to get rid of them. The most effective method of flea control is a two-stage approach: first kill the adult fleas, then control the development of pre-adult fleas. Treat your home with an insect growth regulator spray and an insecticide to kill adult fleas, making sure you cover all carpets, furniture, bedding, hidden crevices, and anywhere else your dog likes to spend time.

Once you've taken care of your home, it's time to treat your dog. Some products are liquid treatments that you squeeze onto your dog's back between the shoulders; others are in pill form, which you give to your dog in his food each month. When placed on the back of the dog's neck, the liquid drops spread throughout the hair and skin to kill the adult fleas. It's best to ask your vet which

Other Vaccines and Treatment

Depending on where you live and your dog's needs, the following ailments and diseases can be treated through your veterinarian.

CONDITION	TREATMENT	PROGNOSIS	RECOMMENDATION
BORDETELLA (KENNEL COUGH)	Keep warm; humidify room; moderate exercise	Highly contagious; rarely fatal in healthy dogs; easily treated	Optional; prevalence varies; vaccine may be linked to acute reactions; low efficacy
FLEA AND TICK	Topical and ingestible	Highly contagious	Highly recommended
HEARTWORM	Arsenical compound; rest; restricted exercise	Widely occurring infections; preventive programs available regionally; successful treatment after early detection	Preventive treatment highly recommended
INTESTINAL WORMS	Dewormer; home medication regimen	Good with prompt treatment	Highly recommended
LYME DISEASE	Antibiotics	Can't completely eliminate the organism, but can be controlled in most cases	Recommended only for dogs with high risk of exposure to deer ticks
PARAINFLUENZA	Rest; humidify room; moderate exercise	Highly contagious; mild; self-limiting; rarely fatal	Optional but recommended; doesn't block infection, but lessens clinical signs
PERIODONTITIS	Dental cleaning; extractions; repair	Excellent, but involves anesthesia	Recommended

medicines are right for fighting your dog's fleas. You can purchase flea remedies from your veterinarian or from a pet-supply store.

Ticks: Ticks are a concern for active dog breeds that like to spend time outdoors. Ticks can spread diseases, such as Lyme disease (borreliosis), which sometimes spread to humans as well. Talk to your vet to find out if ticks are a major concern for your region. He or she will have information for how to protect your German Shepherd Dog and be able to discuss whether the Lyme disease vaccine is in your dog's best interest.

Mites: Regularly check your German Shepherd for ear mites. They can't be seen, but a brown discharge with some odor from the ear is a clear indication that they're there. If you see these telltale signs, go to your veterinarian for a suitable ear treatment.

Know Your Vaccines

The American Veterinary Medical Association (AVMA) recommends certain CORE vaccines for your puppy. These vaccines protect your German Shepherd Dog from diseases that are very dangerous to your puppy, such as canine hepatitis and rabies. Many of these CORE vaccines are mandatory in certain states. The rabies vaccine, for example, is required in all fifty states. Your vet will tell you which vaccinations your puppy needs. You can read more about vaccines on the AVMA website, www.avma.org.

After playing outdoors, check your GSD for ticks or any other hitchhiking pests. If your dog appears to have been bitten by a mosquito, check with your veterinarian as soon as possible on treatment.

Signs to Watch For

It's your job to check your GSD for any changes in his appearance or behavior between his annual visits to the vet.

Things to watch for:
- Has your dog gained a few too many pounds or suddenly lost weight?
- Are his teeth clean and white?
- Is he going to the bathroom more frequently or drinking more water than usual?
- Does he have a hard time going to the bathroom?
- Are there any changes in his appetite?
- Does he appear short of breath, lazy, or overly tired?
- Does he limp or have a hard time walking around?

These can be signs of serious health problems that you should discuss with your vet as soon as they appear. It's especially important for older dogs because even small changes can be a sign of something serious.

Worms: Dogs can also carry internal parasites in the form of worms. Ascarid roundworms are the most common. Tapeworms, although less frequent, can be even more debilitating. Heartworms are transmitted by mosquitoes; they pose a serious health risk for dogs. Discuss preventive treatment with your vet. Some monthly treatments work to protect against heartworm, as well as some of the other common internal parasites.

Depending on where you live, your vet will advise you on the best way to protect your dog from various pests. Owners of outdoorsy breeds like the GSD must consider extra precautions for avoiding ticks and mosquitoes whenever possible. For dogs of all breeds and sizes, however, routine worming is essential throughout your dog's life. But be sure to discuss all parasite-management options with your vet before starting any treatment.

WELL-BEING CHECKS

With today's busy lifestyle, many owners fail to really look at their dogs. They "see" their dogs, but do not think to stop and truly observe them. As a result, they don't notice problems that their dogs may have until they get worse and require more extensive treatment. To avoid this problem with your German Shepherd, watch him for a few minutes every day as he moves around. Look for any hesitation in his gait that could indicate a hip, foot, or leg problem. At least once a week, run your hands all over your dog's body, feeling for lumps or wounds and noting any dry skin or tender places. With GSDs, this means getting your fingers underneath the fur. Look in your dog's ears and mouth, and examine his feet, too. Check around the anus for any swelling or fecal matter. This whole wellness exam takes less than five minutes a day and can prevent suffering and high veterinary costs later.

Spend five minutes everyday and observe your German Shepherd's behavior and movements. You may catch a health problem in its early stages this way.

ALTERNATIVE MEDICINE

There are several alternatives to traditional Western veterinary medicine. Today, a small but growing number of veterinarians have degrees in both traditional and alternative medicine. Some holistic treatments include nutritional therapy, flower essences, herbs, acupuncture and acupressure, therapeutic massage, chiropractic treatment, and homeopathy. Some illnesses are best treated with a combination of traditional and holistic approaches, so if such treatments appeal to you, keep an open mind and work with practitioners who don't automatically reject other methods.

Support Canine Health Research

The American Kennel Club Canine Health Foundation (www.akcchf.org) raises money to support canine health research. The foundation makes grants to fund:

- Identifying the cause(s) of disease
- Earlier, more accurate diagnosis
- Accurate, positive prognosis
- Effective, efficient treatment

The AKC Canine Health Foundation (AKC CHF) also supports educational programs that bring scientists together to discuss their work and develop new collaborations to further advance canine health. The AKC created the AKC Canine Health Foundation in 1995 to raise funds to support canine health research. Each year, the AKC CHF allocates $1.5 million to new canine health research projects.

How You Can Help: If you have an AKC-registered dog, submit his DNA sample (cheek swab or blood sample) to the Canine Health Information Center (CHIC) DNA databank (www.caninehealthinfo.org). Encourage regular health testing by breeders, get involved with your local dog club, and support the efforts to host health education programs. And, if possible, make a donation.

For information, contact the AKC Canine Health Foundation, P.O. Box 900061, Raleigh, NC 27675-9061 or check out the website at www.akcchf.org.

Big dogs like GSDs need regular exercise to stay healthy. Active people make the best GSD owners.

At a Glance ...

Preventive care is the best way to take care of your German Shepherd Dog. Don't wait until he's very ill to go to the veterinarian for help. Take your dog for regular, annual checkups to ensure his health is on track.

For the most up-to-date breed-specific health information, refer to the German Shepherd Dog Club of America website (www.gsdca.org).

Pest control is guaranteed to be a problem for anyone with an active, outdoorsy dog. Your veterinarian will be able to help you combat any parasite from fleas to heartworm.

Keep an eye out for any unusual behavior or other signs of illness, and take your dog to the vet immediately if you're unsure.

CHAPTER TEN

Activities for German Shepherds

If your German Shepherd Dog has learned self-control and is reliable in obeying basic obedience commands, there is a world full of interesting things you can participate in together. Because the German Shepherd is a breed that truly enjoys pleasing his owners, he will happily try any activity he's asked to do. If the result is attention and praise, then the GSD will participate eagerly. The two of you can do anything together, as long as you're both physically capable.

Consider your GSD's conditioning before taking up a new, active hobby. Work up to strenuous activities through daily training and exercise.

Non-organized activities such as hiking and backpacking are excellent choices for the GSD. Be sure to consider your dog's conditioning before any strenuous exercise, such as long-distance jogging (especially while you're riding a bicycle) or mountain hiking, where your dog can become injured. Also pay attention to your dog's foot pads, making sure they are used to walking on rough surfaces before the activity and checking them frequently during your outings. When backpacking, the strong GSD can carry his own food and equipment in a specially-fitted canine backpack. The rule of thumb is that a dog can typically carry one-sixth of his body weight.

Not every GSD will excel at all activities, but as long as you and your dog are enjoying yourselves and getting some physical and mental exercise, it's good enough. Through his intensity of interest and extra willingness to work, your German Shepherd will let you know what activities he most enjoys. And that's the thing he'll shine at, given proper guidance.

ACTIVE IN THE COMMUNITY

Whether they're accompanying their owners to hospitals and care facilities or sniffing through airports for drugs and explosives, German Shepherds love to

A PIECE OF HISTORY

The first German Shepherd Dog was exhibited in America in 1907, when Mira von Offingen (imported by Otto Gross) was shown by H. Dalrymple, of Port Allegheny, Pennsylvania, in the open class at Newcastle and Philadelphia.

GSDs love just about any outdoor activity, and they excel in organized sports like agility, which often include running through weave poles.

help. They're no happier than when given an important job to do with the people they love. The breed's special blend of smarts, sturdiness, and fierce loyalty lends well to work in the community, a service for which we are all grateful.

Therapy Workers

GSDs that enjoy interacting with people can serve as visiting therapy dogs and participate in animal-assisted therapy. If you enlist your friendly German Shepherd's services as a visiting therapy dog, you will go to hospitals and elder care facilities where your dog will gently interact with the residents. These visits are often the highlight of the week for people who miss their own pets, past and present.

Animal-assisted therapy is a much more demanding job, in which the dog and owner work together on a regular basis with a psychologist, psychiatrist, occupational therapist, or physical therapist to help patients reach their goals. The dog's job requirements may vary from things like walking with the patient to help improve ambulation skills to sitting quietly while the patient brushes or strokes him to help improve the patient's emotional well-being, muscular strength, and hand-eye coordination.

In "animal-assisted activities," the dog serves as a focus for entertainment by providing non-threatening and unconditional attention to the patients. In this therapy role, the dog may do things like facilitate play sessions or act as a reading partner to give the patient incentive to read aloud. This type of therapy is not usually very regimented in record keeping or in treatment-goal achievement, instead aimed at providing positive interactions for the patients. Often, you can work directly with a hospital or care facility to bring your dog for therapy

German Shepherds help service our community in many ways, whether as therapy workers, guide dogs, law-enforcement K-9s, or simply friends.

Whether you choose a casual game of fetch or the competitive atmosphere of canine sporting, your GSD will love spending time with you.

Deadly Water

If you take your GSD to places with lakes and ponds in warm seasons, be very cautious about letting him drink the water. Algae is usually harmless, but blue-green algae (tiny water plants) can become toxic under certain conditions. In nutrient-rich lakes, the blue-green algae can "bloom" in abundance; the water becomes cloudy, with a green, yellow, or blue-green hue. The toxic algae may form large floating masses and smell foul.

People or animals who come in contact with toxic blue-green algae can become seriously ill because the toxin attacks the kidneys and liver. In some cases, it has been fatal to animals. Symptoms of algae poisoning vary, ranging from mild skin irritations and vomiting, to severe disorders involving the circulatory, nervous and digestive systems. In extreme cases, the animal may suffer convulsions and die. If your dog ingests blue-green algae, consult a veterinarian as soon as possible. If the algae gets on his coat, wash it off before your dog tries to lick himself.

Activities for German Shepherds

German Shepherds can help patients therapeutically, both helping peoples' physical and emotional well-being.

sessions whenever they need; however, animal-assisted therapy dogs must be approved or certified by a parent organization before they will be allowed into the hospitals and nursing homes.

If you think your GSD would make a great therapy dog, the American Kennel Club can help get you started. There are many programs devoted to canine therapy work. Contact the following organizations for more information to get started.

- **AKC's Canine Good Citizen® program:** Rewarding dogs that have good manners at home and in the community, this two-part program requires dogs to pass a ten-step test to receive a certificate touting the dog's preparedness for positive interaction in your community. It's the first step toward reaching out to others in your community together with your dog. Learn more about the program at www.akc.org/events/cgc.

- **AKC Therapy Dog program:** New to the AKC's list of offerings, this program recognizes all AKC dog-and-owner teams that have volunteered their time and helped people in therapy work. It awards an official AKC Therapy Dog title (AKC ThD) to dogs that have been certified by recognized therapy dog associations and have worked to improve the lives of the people they've visited. Get more information at www.akc.org/akctherapydog.

- **Delta Society:** Matching people with mental and physical disabilities and patients in healthcare facilities together with professionally trained animals, this international nonprofit organization helps to improve patients' health. Learn more about the Delta Society at www.deltasociety.com.

- **Therapy Dogs Inc:** For members involved in animal-assisted volunteer activities, this organization provides registration, support, and insurance. Visit www.therapydogs.com for more information.

- **Therapy Dogs International:** Helping qualified handlers and their therapy dogs visit facilities and institutions where therapy dogs are needed, this nonprofit volunteer group is always looking for a few good dogs. Get more information at www.tdi-dog.org.

K-9 OFFICIALS

Well-trained and extremely loyal, many German Shepherd Dogs serve our community in an official capacity. These canine civic servants help in many ways, from police and detection ("bomb-sniffing") work to search-and-rescue and cadaver discovery. Whatever job, they are revered for their helpfulness in society.

Police dogs (often referred as "K-9 dogs") are trained specifically to assist police and other law-enforcement personnel in their work. German Shepherds are among the most commonly trained breeds for the job. These canine officials are treated with respect and regarded highly by those in the service. It's even a felony in most jurisdictions to intentionally injure or kill a police dog, often punishable with harsher penalties than most other local animal-cruelty laws. Many

Rescue Me

GSDs excel in search and rescue (SAR). Many local and national organizations provide instruction and certification for this very important work. SAR dogs have been invaluable in helping during natural disasters and catastrophes, such as finding missing people and tracking children who've wandered away from home. German Shepherds are among the leading breeds in this field. For more information about SAR dogs, search the National Association for Search and Rescue's page at www.nasar.org/page34/Canine-Search-and-Rescue.

GSDs are one of the most popular K-9 breeds. Police dogs chase/hold suspects, locate missing people, and detect drugs or explosives, among other dangerous job duties.

> **Join the Club**
>
> Consider joining a regional GSD club or the national club, the German Shepherd Dog Club of America (www.gsdca.org). Through these organizations, you can find other owners, participate in GSD gatherings, find information on educational seminars, and ask more experienced owners for advice.

law-enforcement organizations outfit their dogs with bullet-proof vests, and some even make their K-9s sworn officers, complete with police badges and IDs. Any K-9s killed in the line of duty are even bestowed a full police funeral.

EXCELLENCE IN TRAINING

Beyond the everyday exercise options of walking and playing together, your GSD might enjoy spending time with other dogs and people in competitive canine sports. The AKC offers an array of events—from agility to conformation to tracking to herding. Many dogs enjoy sports that test their smarts and athletic prowess, arenas in which the German Shepherd Dog excels. If this sounds like something you think you and your dog would enjoy, there are many ways to get involved.

Puppies aren't allowed in competition because they aren't yet done growing, but once your GSD turns a year old, he should be ready to compete. However, before starting any type of strenuous exercise, talk to your veterinarian to make sure your dog's healthy enough to participate.

Start with classes in a specific sport. If your German Shepherd shows a talent for agility, rally, obedience, or herding, definitely consider competing. The AKC and the German Shepherd Dog Club of America offer competitive events for a variety of sports discussed below. Go to www.akc.org and www.gsdca.org for more information.

Conformation Shows

All GSDs are beautiful, and many are excellent representatives of the breed, but only a very small percentage have the appearance and personality required to win consistently at dog shows. In conformation competitions, the dogs are judged against the AKC's breed standard. The judge's job is to pick the dogs that, on the day of competition, most closely resemble the description in the standard.

Dog shows are not "beauty pageants," but there is a certain degree of subjectivity on the part of the judges, who are impressed by a dog's personality, confidence, and performance on the day. Sometimes the technical conformational excellence comes second to a better trained, dynamic German Shepherd that is telling the judge "Pick me!" If there are two dogs equal in conformational correctness, and one moves around the ring without enthusiasm and looks disinterested when he is stacked for the judge (standing in a show pose for examination), while the other practically sends sparks of energy and proudly gazes back at the judge, of course the latter will win. At the end of the day, the judge's placements simply reflect his or her opinion as to which dogs were the best breed representations offered on that day. Another judge on another day may make different choices.

If your GSD is registered with the AKC and a breeder, a professional handler, or a show judge has evaluated your dog's conformation and believes he is worth showing, then definitely consider exhibiting in conformation competitions. Go to some dog shows and observe how the German Shepherds are presented. After the judging is over, you may have the chance to ask questions of the other GSD owners present. If any of the exhibitors are local, be sure to ask if there are any show-handling instructors or trainers in the area who understand how to present a GSD because the breed requires a very different

James Moses, the most successful German Shepherd Dog handler in competitive conformation, shows at dog a conformation event.

presentation and gaiting style from other breeds. You can find further information about how to get involved in dog shows through the AKC's website at www.akc.org/events/conformation/beginners.cfm.

The German Shepherd is a popular breed, so you'll be competing against specialized handlers and experienced owner-handlers who do a wonderful job of presenting their dogs. To receive the judge's nod, a novice handler's dog must be exceptionally outstanding compared to the rest of the entries, unless that novice has worked extra hard to learn the tricks of handling, grooming, and conditioning used by the consistent winners. But keep in mind: all of those experienced semi-professionals and professionals were once beginners, too.

Obedience Trials

In obedience training, a puppy learns to follow basic cues (*sit*, *down*, *stay*, *come*, etc.), and you learn how to properly give your dog those cues. If your dog's a whiz in his classes, consider involving him in the AKC's obedience trials. The first title a dog can earn is Beginner Novice (BN), then Companion Dog (CD), which entails heeling on and off leash, coming when called, standing still while the judge touches him, and staying in both the *sit* and *down* positions until released by the handler. The next title up is Companion Dog Excellent (CDX), which includes off-leash heeling, longer stays, retrieving and jumping. Tests for the next level, Utility Dog (UD), are all off leash, and include directed retrieving (in which the handler signals the dog to pick up one of three objects), scent discrimination (in which the dog must choose one of several objects the handler has recently touched), and extended *stays* (in which the dog stays still for a determined amount of time until given a cue to release).

Once a dog earns one of these titles, the initials of the title are listed after the dog's name in his pedigree. The AKC also offers an Obedience Trial Champion (OTCH) title for dogs that have earned a UD and received a required number of winning placements in continued competition. Learn more about the AKC's obedience program, the sport's history, its importance, and the obedience titles you can earn at www.akc.org/events/obedience.

Agility Trials

The fast-paced sport of agility is exciting to watch and fun for all dogs to participate in. Agility requires the dog to overcome several obstacles as indicated by his handler, who runs alongside the dog. The winning dog completes the obstacle course in the fastest time and loses the fewest points due to technical mistakes.

Common obstacles in agility are jumps of various forms, teeter-totters, elevated walkways, tunnels, and a set of closely-spaced poles called "weave poles." If the dog takes obstacles without the handler's direction, knocks down a jump, or fails to touch his paws in designated places, he will lose points. Agility training focuses on

Highly intelligent and trainable, German Shepherds can learn to navigate obstacle courses and use their scenting abilities.

positive rewards and encouragement. Active, energetic dogs seem to enjoy the challenge. If your German Shepherd Dog is high-energy, training him in agility can be a wonderful outlet for much of that energy. This type of training also strengthens the owner-dog bond because you must learn to work closely together as a team. Learn more about AKC's agility events at www.akc.org/events/agility.

After any outdoor excursion, make sure to give your GSD a thorough check for any cuts, scrapes, or other injuries.

Rally

If you're looking for an activity that combines the precision of obedience with the fast-paced style of agility, then you should definitely try Rally, the newest AKC sport. Rally was developed after the rally style of auto racing. In this sport, the dog/handler team must navigate through a course made up of directional signs. Each course is unique, to keep competitors on their toes. It's great for first-time competitors or anyone new to companion events, as well as seasoned vets.

If you choose to compete as your dog's handler in this sport, you and your German Shepherd will get to show off your skills together. Similar to obedience trials, this sport shows how well your dog does what you ask of him. But the performance rules for rally are a bit more lax than for obedience, so you can be more relaxed and really have fun with it. On a rally course, you can expect to work your way together with your GSD through ten to twenty stations, each requiring your team to show off some skill. For more information about AKC rally competitions, go to www.akc.org/events/rally.

Tracking

Have you ever watched a movie in which a dog is sent out to find a lost person? What the dog is doing is called tracking. In tracking events, dogs show off their natural ability to follow the scent of a particular person.

In tracking competition, a stranger will lay (create) a track by walking along a pre-determined path. It's then up to the dog to follow this path through to the

The AKC Code of Sportsmanship

- Sportsmen respect the history, traditions, and integrity of the sport of purebred dogs.
- Sportsmen commit themselves to values of fair play, honesty, courtesy, and vigorous competition, as well as winning and losing with grace.
- Sportsmen refuse to compromise their commitment and obligation to the sport of purebred dogs by injecting personal advantage or consideration into their decisions or behavior.
- The sportsman judge judges only on the merits of the dogs and considers no other factors.
- The sportsman judge or exhibitor accepts constructive criticism.
- The sportsman exhibitor declines to enter or exhibit under a judge where it might reasonably appear that the judge's placements could be based on something other than the merits of the dogs.
- The sportsman exhibitor refuses to compromise the impartiality of a judge.
- The sportsman respects the American Kennel Club's bylaws, rules, regulations, and policies governing the sport of purebred dogs.
- Sportsmen find that vigorous competition and civility are not inconsistent and are able to appreciate the merit of their competition and the efforts of competitors.
- Sportsmen welcome, encourage, and support newcomers to the sport.
- Sportsmen will deal fairly with all those who trade with them.
- Sportsmen are willing to share honest and open appraisals of both the strengths and weaknesses of their breeding stock.
- Sportsmen spurn any opportunity to take personal advantage of positions offered or bestowed upon them.
- Sportsmen always consider as paramount the welfare of their dogs.
- Sportsmen refuse to embarrass the sport, the American Kennel Club, or themselves while taking part in the sport.

When tracking, the German Shepherd's strong instincts kick in. This is what helps the breed to also excel in detection and search-and-rescue.

end. While tracking, the dog is on a harness and long leash, which the handler may hold but cannot use to direct the dog. Usually, the handler will then let the dog smell an object with the tracklayer's scent, indicate to the dog where the track starts, and follow along behind him. In competition, the dog is required to continually keep working at sniffing out the track without becoming distracted by wildlife, other dogs, or anything else along the way. If the dog wanders off course and does not immediately return, he is disqualified.

Tracking is great exercise for your GSD and another chance for the two of you to work together in a fun environment. Go to www.akc.org/events/tracking for more information about the AKC's tracking events.

Herding

There are two types of AKC herding events: competitive and noncompetitive. The purpose of noncompetitive herding tests is to offer herding-breed owners a standardized gauge by which a dog's basic instinct and trainability are measured. The purpose of the competitive herding trial program is to preserve and develop the herding skills inherent in herding breeds and to demonstrate that they can perform the useful functions for which they were originally bred. Although herding trials are artificial simulations of pastoral or farm situations, they are still standardized tests to measure and develop the characteristics of the herding breeds.

Dogs must have training and prior exposure to livestock before entering tests or trials. Both parent and local clubs often provide opportunities for such training and exposure.

The initial assessment is called an Instinct Test. A dog doesn't need any training before entering this class and may be handled by the judge, his owner, or a designated handler. In a herding event, the judge evaluates the dog's ability to move and control livestock by fetching or driving.

Look for activities the entire family can participate in—they're fun, promote exercise, and they strengthen the human-animal bond.

German Shepherd Dogs are natural herders, and with a little encouragement and training, your GSD could be reliving his ancestors' past, moving sheep on an open field. For more information about AKC herding events, log on to www.akc.org/events/herding.

STAY ACTIVE, HAVE FUN

Regardless of what activity you decide to get involved in with your German Shepherd, just make sure you stay active! Your GSD will get restless without it. Take him for daily walks, go for a run at the beach, play catch at a park—just remember to have fun with your dog, and he'll become a loving companion for life.

Get the Kids Involved

The American Kennel Club shows its commitment to supporting young people in their interest in purebred dogs by awarding thousands of dollars of scholarships to those competing in Junior Showmanship. The scholarships range from $1,000 to $5,000 and are based on a student's academic achievements and his or her history with purebred dogs. Learn more at www.akc.org/kids_juniors.

At a Glance ...

Because the German Shepherd is both highly trainable and very active, your dog will need plenty of exercise and can excel in many sports and other activities, if you invest the time in it.

....

Conformation, agility, tracking, herding, and obedience are just a few of the events that the American Kennel Club offers for German Shepherd Dogs and their owners.

....

As a herder by nature, the GSD is naturally inclined to this sport. However, if you lack the space and livestock, the AKC and the GSD's national parent club can provide avenues to allow your dog to flex his herding muscles.

....

Regardless of what activity you choose to do with your dog, the important thing is that you both have fun and stay healthy together for years to come.

Resources

BOOKS

The American Kennel Club's Meet the Breeds: Dog Breeds from A to Z (Irvine, California: BowTie Press, 2010) The ideal puppy buyer's guide, this book provides all the information you need to know about each breed currently recognized by the AKC.

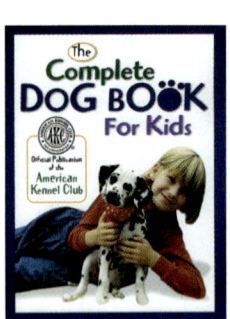

The Complete Dog Book, 20th edition (New York: Ballantine Books, 2006) This official publication of the AKC, first published in 1929, includes the complete histories and breed standards of 153 recognized breeds, as well as information on general care and the dog sport.

The Complete Dog Book for Kids (New York: Howell Book House, 1996) Specifically geared toward young people, this official publication of the AKC presents 149 breeds and varieties, as well as introductory owners' information.

Citizen Canine: Ten Essential Skills Every Well-Mannered Dog Should Know by Mary R. Burch, PhD (Freehold, New Jersey: Kennel Club Books, 2010) This official AKC publication is the definitive guide to the AKC's Canine Good Citizen program, recognized as the gold standard of behavior for dogs, with more than half a million dogs trained.

DOGS: The First 125 Years of the American Kennel Club (Freehold, New Jersey: Kennel Club Books, 2009) This official AKC publication presents an authoritative complete history of the AKC, including detailed information not found in any other volume.

Dog Heroes of September 11: A Tribute to America's Search and Rescue Dogs, 10th anniversary edition, by Nona Kilgore Bauer (Irvine, California: BowTie Press, 2011) The only publication to salute the canines that served the nation in the recovery missions following the terrorists' attacks on America, this book serves as a lasting tribute to these noble American heroes.

The Original Dog Bible: The Definitive Source for All Things Dog, 2nd edition, by Kristin Mehus-Roe (Irvine, California: BowTie Press, 2009) This 831-page magnum opus includes more than 250 breed profiles, hundreds of color photographs, and a wealth of information on every dog topic imaginable—thousands of practical tips on grooming, training, care, and much more.

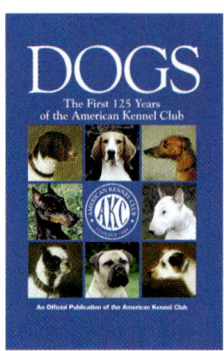

PERIODICALS

American Kennel Club Gazette

Every month since 1889, serious dog fanciers have looked to the *Gazette* for authoritative advice on training, showing, breeding, and canine health. Each issue includes the breed columns section, written by experts from the respective breed clubs. Now only available electronically.

AKC Family Dog

This is a bi-monthly magazine for the dog lover whose special dog is "just a pet." Helpful tips, how-tos, and features are written in an entertaining and reader-friendly format. It's a lifestyle magazine for today's busy families who want to enjoy the most rewarding, mutually happy relationship with their canine companions.

Dog Fancy

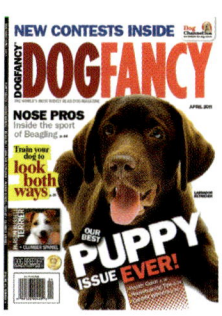

The world's most widely read dog magazine, *Dog Fancy* celebrates dogs and the people who love them. Each monthly issue includes info on cutting-edge medical developments, health and fitness (with a focus on prevention, treatment, and natural therapy), behavior and training, travel and activities, breed profiles and dog news, issues and trends for purebred and mixed-breed dog owners. The magazine informs, inspires, and entertains readers while promoting responsible dog ownership. Throughout its more than forty-year history, *Dog Fancy* has garnered numerous honors, including being named the Best All-Breed Magazine by the Dog Writers Association of America.

Dog World

With more than ninety-five years of tradition as the top magazine for active people with active dogs, *Dog World* provides authoritative, valuable, and entertaining content to the community of

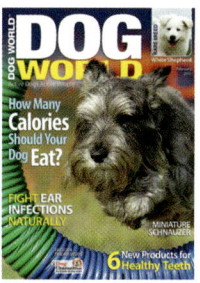

serious dog enthusiasts and participants, including breeders; conformation exhibitors; obedience, agility, herding, and field trial competitors; veterinarians; groomers; and trainers. This monthly magazine is the resource to turn to for up-to-date information about canine health, advanced training, holistic and homeopathic methods, breeding, and conformation and performance sports.

Dogs in Review

For more than fifteen years, *Dogs in Review* has showcased the finest dogs in the U.S. and from around the world. The emphasis has always been on strong editorial content, with input from distinguished breeders, judges, and handlers worldwide. This global perspective distinguishes this monthly publication from its competitors—no other North American dog-show magazine gathers together so many international experts to enlighten and entertain its readership.

Dogs USA

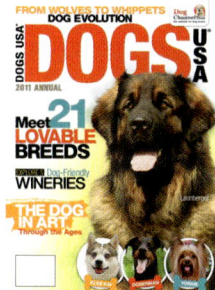

Dogs USA is an annual lifestyle magazine published by the editors of *Dog Fancy* that covers all aspects of the dog world: culture, art, history, travel, sports, and science. It also profiles breeds to help prospective owners choose the best dogs for their future needs, such as a potential show champion, super service dog, great pet, or competitive star.

Natural Dog

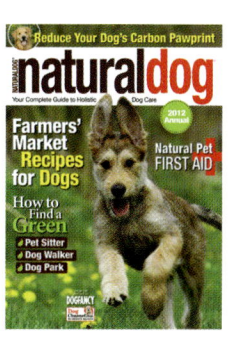

Natural Dog is the annual magazine dedicated to giving a dog a natural lifestyle. From nutritional choices to grooming to dog-supply options, this publication helps readers make the transition from traditional

to natural methods. The magazine also explores the array of complementary treatments available for today's dogs: acupuncture, massage, homeopathy, aromatherapy, and much more. *Natural Dog* appears as an annual publication and also as the flip side of *Dog Fancy* magazine four times a year (in February, May, August, and November).

Puppies USA

Also from the editors of *Dog Fancy,* this annual magazine offers essential information for all new puppy owners. *Puppies USA* is lively and informative, including advice on general care, nutrition, grooming and training techniques for all puppies, whether purebred or mixed breed, adopted, rescued, or purchased. In addition, it offers family fun through quizzes, contests, and much more. An extensive breeder directory is included.

WEBSITES

www.akc.org

The American Kennel Club's (AKC's) website is an excellent starting point for researching dog breeds and learning about puppy care. The site lists hundreds of breeders, along with basic information about breed selection and basic care. The site also has links to the national breed club of every AKC-recognized breed; breed-club sites offer plenty of detailed breed information, as well as lists of member breeders. In addition, you can find the AKC National Breed Club Rescue Network at www.akc.org/breeds/rescue.cfm. If looking for purebred puppies, go to www.puppybuyerinfo.com for AKC classifieds and parent club referrals.

www.dogchannel.com

Dog Channel is "the website for dog lovers," where hundreds of thousands of visitors each month find extensive information on breeds, training, health and nutrition, puppies, care, activities, and more. Interactive features include forums, Dog College, games, puzzles, and Club Dog, an exclusive free club where dog lovers can create blogs for their pets and earn points to buy products. DogChannel is the definitive one-stop site for all things dog.

www.meetthebreeds.com

The official website of the AKC Meet the Breeds® event, hosted by the American Kennel Club in the Jacob Javits Center in New York City this fall. The first Meet the Breeds event took place in 2009. The website includes information on every recognized breed of dog and cat, alphabetically listed, as well as the breeders, demonstration facilitators, sponsors, and vendors participating in the annual event.

AKC AFFILIATES

The AKC Museum of the Dog, established in 1981, is located in St. Louis, Missouri, and houses the world's finest collection of art devoted to the dog.

The **AKC Humane Fund** promotes the joy and value of responsible and productive pet ownership through education, outreach, and grant-making. Monies raised may fund grants to organizations that teach responsible pet ownership; provide for the health and well-being of all dogs; and preserve and celebrate the human-animal bond and the evolutionary relationship between dogs and humankind.

The **American Kennel Club Companion Animal Recovery (CAR) Corporation** is dedicated to reuniting lost microchipped and tattooed pets with their owners. AKC CAR maintains a permanent-identification database and provides lifetime recovery services 24 hours a day, 365 days a year, for all animal species. Millions of pets are enrolled in the program. Coordinators have recovered hundreds of thousands of pets since the program's inception in 1995.

The American Kennel Club Canine Health Foundation (AKC CHF), Inc. is the largest foundation in the world to fund canine-only health studies for purebred and mixed-breed dogs. More than $22 million has been allocated in health-research funds to more than 500 studies conducted to help dogs live longer, healthier lives. Go to www.akcchf.org.

AKC PROGRAMS

The Canine Good Citizen Program (CGC) was established in 1989 and is designed to recognize dogs that have good manners at home and in the community. This rapidly growing, nationally recognized program stresses responsible dog ownership for owners and basic training and good manners for dogs. All dog that pass the ten-step Canine Good Citizen test receive a certificate from the American Kennel Club.

The **AKC S.T.A.R. Puppy Program** is designed to get dog owners and their puppies off to a good start and is aimed at loving dog owners who have taken the time to attend basic obedience classes with their puppies. After completing a six-week training course, the puppy must pass the AKC S.T.A.R. Puppy test, which evaluates Socialization, Training, Activity, and Responsibility.

The **AKC Therapy Dog** program recognizes all American Kennel Club dogs and their owners who have given their time and helped people by volunteering as a therapy dog and owner team. The AKC Therapy Dog program is an official AKC title awarded to dogs who have worked to improve the lives of the people they have visited. The AKC Therapy Dog title (AKC ThD) is an AKC title that can be earned by dogs who have been certified by recognized therapy dog organizations. Visit www.akc.org/akctherapydog.

Resources **125**

Index

A
Adenovirus-2 98
Adjustable collar 42
Agility 114
    trials 15, 116
Aggression 48, 49
AKC
    Approved CGC Evaluator 92
    Canine Good Citizen
        Program 60, 95, 112
    Canine Good Citizen test 92, 94
    Canine Health Foundation 104
    Code of Sportsmanship 118
    Companion Animal Recovery
    Canine Support and
        Relief Fund 32, 49
    Eukanuba National
        Championship 86
    Meet the Breeds 24
    Registration 38
    Responsible Dog Ownership
        Days 32, 60
    S.T.A.R. Puppy 59, 60, 95
    Therapy Dog Program 112
    Therapy Dog Title 112
Alpha 55
Alsatian Shepherd 31
American Veterinary Medical
    Association 101
Animal-assisted therapy 110
Anxiety 46
Association of American Feed
    Control Officials 74

B
Backpacking 108
Barking 48
Bathing 79, 80
Bedding 43
Bedtime training 65
Biting 56
    aggressive 56
    playful 51
Bloat 5
Blue-green algae 111
Bomb and drug detection 8
Bordetella (Kennel Cough) 100
Breed standard 16, 18, 25, 26, 114
Breeder 28
    experience 33
    questions 33
    visit 37

Brushing 9, 44, 78, 79
Bullet 89

C
Canine
    Eye Registration
        Foundation (CERF) 36
    Good Citizen Program 32, 34
    Good Citizen Test 92
    Health Information Center
        DNA Databank 104
Carbohydrates 74
Certified Pedigree 38
Ch. Altana's Mystique 18
Ch. Etzel v.d. Ettersburg 9
Champion 30
Chewing 58
Child interaction 48
Choosing a Veterinarian 98
Coat 9-10, 20
Comb 44, 78
Come command 58, 91, 115
Commands 88
Companion Dog 30
Conformation 114
    shows 18, 114
Conditioning 115
CORE Vaccines 98, 101
Corporal Lee Duncan 12
Crate 64, 65, 68
    duration 70
    training 64
Cues 90
    basic 115
    poisoned 90

D
Dam (mother) 31, 36, 54
Delta Society 112
Dental care 78, 79, 82
Diarrhea 74
Diet 72
    changes 74
    for adults 76
    for performance dogs 76
    for puppies 75
Distemper 98
Dog park 50
DOGNY program 8
Down command 90, 115
Driving 12

E
Ear care 80, 84
Elbow dysplasia 35
Elimination 46
Exercise 58, 72, 77, 108
    pens 69

F
Farm dogs 52
Fats 74
Fear-biting 48
Fleas 99, 100
Food 42
    bowls 42
    canned 74
    dry (kibble) 74, 75
    rewards 89
    soft-moist 74
Free-feeding 77

G
Games 60
Gates 69
German Shepherd Dog Club of
    America 18, 33, 35, 75, 99, 114
German Shepherd Rescue
    Association, Inc. 33
GPS collar 43
Grooming 9, 20, 72, 79, 115
    shopping list 78
    routine 79
Growling 48
Guard dogs 52
Guarding livestock 8
Guiding the blind 8

H
Handling 115
Health
    check 84
    concerns 98
    screening 35
Heat cycles 39
Heel command 56, 94
Hektor von Linkshein 22
Herding 12, 114, 119
    dog 12, 50
    group 6, 19, 20
    instincts 38
    livestock 8
    test 30
Hereditary health problems 99

Hero dogs 8
Hip dysplasia 35
Hollywood Dog Training
    School 65
Hollywood movie stunt dogs 52
Home
    care 72
    introduction 46
Homemade food 74
House training 62, 64, 66, 67
Human introductions 50

I
Identification tag 43
Instinct Test 119

J
Junior Showmanship 120

K
K-9 dogs 113

L
Large-breed puppy formula 42
Leash 42
Loose-leash walking 93
Lyme Disease 100

M
Military dogs 52
Minerals 72, 74
Mites 101
Mustering 12

N
Nail care 79, 82
National Breed Club 20
National parent club ... 18, 33, 35, 75,
    .... 99, 114
National Specialty Show 75
Negative reinforcement 66
Neutering 39
Nutrients 72

O
Obedience 114
    classes 50
    commands 60
    lessons 39
    training 54, 88, 95, 115
    trials 15, 115
    trial champions 52, 116
Orthopedic Foundation for
    Animals (OFA) 30, 35
Osteochondritis dissecans
    (OCD) 36
Owner Suitability 24

P
Pack mentality 55
Paper training 67
Parainfluenze 100
Parvovirus-2 98
Pawing 51
Pedigree 30, 37
Periodontitis 100
Personal space 70
Personality 20, 38
Pet hair dryer 78
Pet Partners, Inc. 24
Play 58, 60
Police dogs 10, 31, 52, 113
Potty
    command 67
    training 62
Positive reinforcement 54, 88
Proteins 74
Puppy
    gates 69
    proofing 40, 45, 69
    training class 50
Purebred dogs 6, 30, 32

Q
Queen Switzerland 19

R
Rabies 8, 101
Rally 114, 117
Registration 32
    certificate 31, 38
    form 30
    papers 37
Responsible Dog Owner's
    pledge 34
Rescue 20, 33
Rin Tin Tin 8, 65, 89
"Rinty" 2
Routine 58, 67

S
Sales contract 37
Search and rescue 8, 52, 113
    National Association for 113
September 11th 6, 8, 86
Service dog 8
Shampoo 78
Shedding 9
Sheep herder 10, 12
Show dogs 52
Signs of ill health 102
Sire (father) 31, 36
Sit command 56, 90, 115
Socialization 48
Spaying 39

Stay command 56, 91, 115
Strongheart 8, 12, 89
Supplies 42

T
Tartar 82
Temperament ..18, 27, 36, 38, 50, 55
    test 36
Tending 12
The Seeing Eye 23
Therapy dogs 110
Therapy Dogs, Inc. 112
Therapy Dogs International 12
Ticks 100, 101
Tone of Voice 58
Toys 44
Tracking 15, 117
Trainability 20, 88
Training 8, 50
    keys 58
    records 93

U
Up command 56

V
Vaccination schedule 37
Verein für Deutsche
    Schäferhunde 22
Veterinary checkup 84, 102
Vitamins 72, 74
Vomiting 74

W
Weight management 75, 77
Wire crate 43, 64
Word association 56, 66
Working dogs 8, 23
Worms 102
    heartworms 100, 102
    intestinal 100
    tapeworms 102

AMERICAN KENNEL CLUB

Advocating for the purebred dog as a family companion, advancing canine health and well-being, working to protect the rights of all dog owners and promoting responsible dog ownership, the **American Kennel Club:**

Sponsors more than **22,000 sanctioned events** annually including conformation, agility, obedience, rally, tracking, lure coursing, earthdog, herding, field trial, hunt test, and coonhound events

Features a **10-step Canine Good Citizen® program** that rewards dogs who have good manners at home and in the community

Has reunited more than **400,000** lost pets with their owners through the AKC Companion Animal Recovery - visit **www.akccar.org**

Created and supports the AKC Canine Health Foundation, which funds research projects using the more than **$22 million** the AKC has donated since 1995 - visit **www.akcchf.org**

Joins **animal lovers** through education, outreach and grant-making via the AKC Humane Fund - visit **www.akchumanefund.org**

We're more than champion dogs. We're the dog's champion.

www.akc.org